Asian Journal of Pentecostal Studies
ISSN 0118-8534
Vol. 19, No. 1 (February 2016)

Editor
David M. Johnson

Editorial Board: Simon Chan (Trinity Theological College, Singapore), Paul Elbert (Pentecostal Theological Seminary, USA), Gordon D. Fee (Regent College, Canada), Peter Kuzmic (Gordon-Conwell Theological Seminary, USA), Wonsuk Ma (Oxford Centre for Mission Studies, UK), Russell P. Spittler (Fuller Theological Seminary, USA), Vinson Synan (Regent University, USA)

Book Review Editor: Teresa Chai

Editorial Committee: Lindsay Crabtree, Kaye Dalton, Debbie Johnson, Frank McNelis, Jon Smith, Kim Snider, Donna Swinford and Melanie Tucker

Layout Editor: Mil Santos

ASIAN JOURNAL OF PENTECOSTAL STUDIES is published twice per year (February and August) by the Faculty of Asia Pacific Theological Seminary, P.O. Box 377, Baguio City 2600, Philippines. Part or whole of the current and previous issues may be available through the internet (http://www.apts.edu/ajps). Views expressed in the *Journal* reflect those of the authors and reviewers, and not the views of the editors, the publisher, or the participating institutions.

© *Asia Pacific Theological Seminary, 2016*
Copyright is waived where reproduction of material from this *Journal* is required for classroom use or course work by students.

PARTICIPATING INSTITUTIONS: Educational or research institutions that are interested in participating in the *Journal* ministry are encouraged to write to the *Journal* office. The following are participating institutions of the Journal:

Central Bible College, Tokyo, Japan (Dr. Koichi Kitano)
Asia LIFE University, Daejon, Korea (Dr. Yeol-Soo Eim)
International Theological Institute, Seoul, Korea (Dr. Sam-Hwan Kim)

THE *JOURNAL SEEKS TO PROVIDE A FORUM*: To encourage serious theological thinking and articulation by Pentecostals/Charismatics in Asia; to promote interaction among Asian Pentecostals/Charismatics and dialogue with other Christian traditions; to stimulate creative contextualization of the Christian faith; and to provide a means for Pentecostals/Charismatics to share their theological reflections.

MANUSCRIPTS AND BOOK REVIEWS submitted for consideration should be sent to *Asian Journal of Pentecostal Studies*, P.O. Box 377, Baguio City 2600, Philippines (fax: 63-74 442-6378; E-mail: apts@agmd.org). Manuscripts and book reviews should be typed double-spaced. Manuscripts should conform in style to the 7th Edition of Kate L. Turabian, *A Manual for Writers of Term Papers, Theses, and Dissertations*. An additional style guide will be sent upon request. The *Journal* encourages contributors to submit an electronic copy prepared through a popular world processor mailed in a Windows-compatible disk or sent as an email attachment.

BOOK FOR REVIEW: Send to the *Journal* Office.

CORRESPONDENCE: Subscription correspondence and notification of change of address should be sent to the subscription office or email to: facultysec@gmail.com.

THIS PERIODICAL IS INDEXED in *Religion index One: Periodicals*, the *index* to books Review in religion, Religion Indexes: Ten Subset on CD-ROM, and the ATLA Religion Database on CD-ROM, published by the American Theological Library Association, 250 S. Wacker Dr., 16th Floor., Chicago, IL 60606 USA, email: atla@atla.com, http://www.atla.com/.

Printed by Wipf and Stock Publishers, 199 W. 8th Ave., Eugene, OR 97401. www.wipfandstock.com. ISBN: 978-1-5326-3679-0

Asian Journal of Pentecostal Studies

Volume 19, Number 1 (March 2016)

EDITORIAL

Dave Johnson Living Out the Counter-Cultural Values of the Kingdom of God	1-2

ARTICLES

Al Tizon Preaching for Whole Life Stewardship	3-15
Al Tizon Preaching for *Shalom*: Life and Peace	17-29
Aldrin M. Peñamora Eucharistic Justice: A Christ-Centered Response to the Bangsamoro Question in the Philippines	31-44
Ivan Satyavrata Power to the Poor: Towards a Pentecostal Theology of Social Engagement	45-57
Yuri Phanon Is She a Sinful Woman or a Forgiven Woman? An Exegesis of Luke 7:36-50 Part I	59-71
Yuri Phanon Is She a Sinful Woman or a Forgiven Woman? An Exegesis of Luke 7:36-50 Part II	73-84

BOOK REVIEW

David Im Seok Kang Richard Averbeck, *Reading Genesis 1:2:* *An Evangelical Conversation*	85-87

R.G. dela Cruz   88-90
  Chas. H. Barfoot, *Aimee Semple McPherson
  and the Making of Modern Pentecostalism*

Robert P. Menzies   91-93
  Lian Xi, *Redeemed by Fire: The Rise of Popular
  Christianity in Modern China*

CONTRIBUTORS   94

Living Out the Counter-Cultural Values of the Kingdom of God

This theme could be said to cover all aspects of life and Al Tizon's two articles, which lead off this edition, fit within that framework. However, the application of his two articles merges with the focus of the remaining four articles in that they have strong ramifications for ministry among the poor, oppressed and disenfranchised of today's world—the segments of society from which the vast majority of Pentecostals and Charismatics are drawn.

In the first of Al Tizon's two articles, he calls us to whole life stewardship, a discipleship concept that goes well beyond money. From coins to creation preservation, he challenges us to be focused on Kingdom values in all aspects of life, looking for ways to give away our time, talent and treasure rather than using it on ourselves. In his second article, he takes us deep into the Hebrew concept of *shalom*, walking in God's peace in all aspects of life. One need not assent to his pacifism to agree that there is much to be said for the concept of "waging peace," whether it is in personal relationships, the war on terror or in resolving legitimate international disputes between nations without resorting to arms.

In his insightful paper on the Muslim/"Christian" conflict in Mindanao, the large island in the southern Philippines, Filipino scholar Aldrin Peñamora, who currently serves as the Research Manager for Muslim/Christian relations under the Philippine Council of Evangelical churches, follows the idea of *shalom* as it regards to the Muslim population on that war torn island. In this case, peace will be achieved through addressing the issues of the injustices of the past. He presents his thoughts within the theological and ethical framework of the Eucharist and calls all of us to follow Christ's example by laying down our lives for others in order to achieve peace and justice for all.

Ivan Satyavrata than explains why Pentecostalism has had such an appeal to the poor, stating that "the Pentecostal message is very good news among the poor: it answers their immediate felt needs and provides powerful spiritual impetus and community support for a better life." He goes on to add that "the genius of Pentecostalism has thus been its relevance to the powerless—its ability to penetrate the enslaving power structures of the socially and economically marginalized." This is an excellent example of the well-known concept of redemption and lift that can be seen in the lives of Christ followers all over the world.

Tizon's and Peñamora's articles were originally presented at the 23rd William W. Menzies Lectureship held on the APTS Baguio campus in January, 2015. Satyavrata's article is a chapter in a book entitled *Pentecostals and the Poor: Reflections From India*, that our own APTS Press will be publishing in the next few months.

Yuri Phanon's two part article, a Greek exegesis paper on Luke 7:36-50, presents an interesting and insightful alternate interpretation to the story of Jesus, Simon the Pharisee and the uninvited woman of low repute at Simon's home. Rejecting the traditional interpretation on the text on exegetical grounds, Phanon holds that the woman had already been forgiven by Christ before she ever set foot in Simon's house and that she came to express her love and gratitude to Jesus for what he had already done. She also does an excellent job of contrasting how this woman responded to Jesus in a respectful, worshipful manner as opposed to the indifferent way in which Simon received him. In doing so, the woman of low estate is more highly esteemed than Simon who, because of his status as a Pharisee, was the one considered "respectable" by Jewish society. Phanon concludes by calling us to be like Jesus in our relationships with those who are not like us.

I hope you enjoy this edition. As always, please feel free to contact me through our website, www.apts.edu.

Your partner in the gospel,

Dave Johnson, D.Miss
Managing Editor

Preaching for Whole Life Stewardship[1]

Al Tizon

Challenging the Global Dream

Lord, help us to remember that all that we have is yours. We commit not just what has been collected in these [offering] plates, but also what we've collected in our bank accounts, our homes, and our properties to your purposes and to your glory. Amen.

This simple prayer, dedicating the tithes and offerings of the people of God, contains necessary elements toward an accurate understanding of biblical stewardship.

Stewardship is not a popular subject. As Scott Rodin quips, "Pastors do not like to preach about it, nor do parishioners like to hear about it; few people write about it and even less read about it."[2] Its unpopularity has to do with the unfortunate fact that people, of which Christians are no exception, believe that their wealth is theirs to do with it what they deem best for their lives. The pursuit of the good life of upward mobility, comfort, security and luxury has spread well beyond the western nations and affected many Asian countries as well and many have been culturally conditioned to believe that this domain belongs privately to each person or church, and that they have the right to do whatever they please with their hard earned wealth. In America, where I live and serve, this is known as pursuing the "American Dream."

---

[1] Adapted from *Missional Preaching: Engage, Embrace, Transform* by Al Tizon, copyright © 2012 by Judson Press. Used by permission of Judson Press. It was also one of the lectures given at the 2015 William Menzies Lectureship, Asia Pacific Theological Seminary in Baguio City, Philippines.

[2] R. Scott Rodin, *Stewards in the Kingdom: A Theology of Life in All Its Fullness* (Downers Grove, IL: IVP, 2000), 9.

This article is written with a specific audience in mind—ministers who primarily serve and preach to Christians and churches with means, wherever they might be, because the American Dream has now become the "Global Dream."[3] Now more than ever, the church around the world, especially those blessed with abundance, needs a fresh and powerful sense of authentic, biblical stewardship. And a certain type of preaching—missional preaching—has an integral part to play in this.

Biblical stewardship not only challenges the privatization of wealth that fortifies the Dream; it challenges the Dream itself by way of the gospel. It threatens what people (again, Christians are no exception) have been taught to be their basic inalienable right, their sense of entitlement. As Christians, it is difficult to be confronted with the possibility that perhaps in the virtually sub-conscious pursuit of the Dream, we have become greedy, materialistic, and consumerist; that perhaps we have taken the culture's cues and have chosen mammon over God (Matt. 6:24). Such thoughts—which get at the heart of biblical stewardship—prick, disturb, and anger good Christian people. So most ministers steer clear of the subject; either that or they reduce stewardship to the management of the church budget and its facilities.

Missional preachers, however, understand and teach biblical stewardship, helping God's people to view and use resources available to them for the advancement of the kingdom. By doing so, the church takes on the Global Dream. For example in America, mega-church pastor David Platt has called not just his congregation but the American church as a whole to take the radical implications of the gospel seriously, to be part of what he calls "the Radical Experiment," which reflects the essence of biblical stewardship. In prophetic fashion, Platt challenges God's people (himself included):

> I dare you to test the claims contained in the gospel, maybe in a way you have never done before. I invite you to see if radical obedience to the commands of Christ is more meaningful, more fulfilling, and more gratifying than the American [Global] Dream. And I guarantee that if you complete this experiment, you will possess an insatiable desire

---

[3]F. Albert Tizon, "Revisiting the Mustard Seed: The Filipino Evangelical Church in the Age of Globalization," *Phronesis* 6/1 (1999), 3ff.

to spend the rest of your life in radical abandonment to Christ for his glory in all the world.[4]

Such preaching at The Church at Brook Hills—Platt's congregation in Birmingham, Alabama USA—has taken its members into a wonderfully new and radical direction. From blindly embracing the church growth theology of the mega-church, which can be viewed as "the American Church Dream," to praying for the needs of the world and sacrificing what they have in the service of the spiritually and materially poor, the Church at Brook Hills has begun to practice biblical stewardship.[5]

From Coins to Creation: Whole Life Stewardship

Biblical stewardship is whole life stewardship.[6] Far from its common reduction to staying in the black in the church's annual budget, stewardship entails all that has been given to us, from the earth's abundant resources to spiritual and material blessings to our relationships to even life itself. "Nothing is left outside the realm of stewardship," claims pastor-teacher Bedru Hussein, "We are completely God's, including what we are and what we have."[7]

Hussein's words point to the essence of whole life stewardship—namely, that nothing ultimately belongs to us, but in fact belongs to God, the Creator and Redeemer of all things. To be a steward then is to be entrusted by God to care for, manage, and cultivate all that is God's. This includes everything, from our financial holdings to the environment and everything in between. From coins to creation, we have been called to be good stewards as an integral part of authentic

---

[4]David Platt, *Radical: Taking Back Your Faith from the American Dream* (Colorado Springs, CO: Multnomah, 2010), 184.

[5]To learn about the Radical Experiment, see "A Radical Proposal," http://www/brookhills.org/ media/series/the-radical-experiment-2010/ and "The Radical Experiment 2010," http://www.brookhills.org/ media/series/the-radical-experiment-2010/ (accessed 23 November 2010).

[6]I first encountered the term "whole life stewardship" in the works of Tom Sine, which include *The New Conspirators: Creating the Future One Mustard Seed at a Time* (Downers Grove, IL: IVP, 2008), 243-252 and the earlier *Why Settle for More and Miss the Best?* (Waco, TX: Word, 1987), 142-150.

[7]Bedru Hussein and Lynn Miller, *Stewardship for All?* (Intercourse, PA: Good Books, 2006), 11.

Christian discipleship. What would happen if Christians truly believed that they have simply been entrusted with God's abundant wealth? What would happen if we truly believed that our homes, our cars, our clothes, our cash were in fact *not* ours, but God's? Internalizing this sense of God's ultimate ownership undergirds what it means to be a biblical steward.

Traits of a Biblical Steward

A Careful View of Wealth

Certain traits accompany biblical stewards. First, they develop a careful view of wealth; they do not automatically equate prosperity with good. Contrary to the claims of the prosperity gospel, one of the most insidious "Christian" versions of the Global Dream, wealth does not always indicate divine blessing. In fact, in light of Jesus' teaching that it is harder for a camel to go through the eye of a needle than for a rich person to enter the kingdom of God (Matt. 19:24; Mark 10:25; Luke 18:25), wealth might be a bad thing, a dangerous thing, a thing that impedes our salvation. Social ethicist Robert Franklin asserts that "the gospel of prosperity is a competitor to authentic Christianity. . ."[8] Indeed, the insatiable pursuit of prosperity (which at the end of the day is nothing less than the love of money that Paul warns us against in 1 Tim. 6:10) can deceptively place us at odds with the gospel. To become rich as the pinnacle of success makes total sense in the secular utopia of the Global Dream, but in light of biblical stewardship where wealth might even be a liability, it makes no sense at all.

Furthermore, a careful view of wealth dispels the notion that the assets and possessions we do have can be used primarily for own personal ends (read: we can do anything we want with our money). As *entrusted* wealth, we would in fact be careful to use it at the very least for things not contrary to the kingdom of God, at best, for purposes that advance the kingdom's agenda. Tom Sine asks with prophetic hope, "Can you imagine the difference it might make if we in the Western church decided to steward all our resources in ways that intentionally

---

[8]Robert M. Franklin, *Crisis in the Village: Restoring Hope in African American Communities* (Minneapolis, MN: Fortress, 2007), 118.

seek to advance God's purposes first instead of prioritizing our own needs and wants?"[9] This attitude flies in the face of viewing our wealth first and foremost as the means for personal advancement, comfort and recreation.

Kingdom Generosity

Such a careful view of wealth leads to a second trait of biblical stewards—namely, kingdom generosity. Which is positively ironic: in our cautious posture toward the prosperity that may come our way, our eyes begin to open to the vast needs around the world and as a result become lavishly generous. How can we become otherwise in light of the world's poor? According to *Global Issues*' "Poverty Facts and Stats:"

- At least 80% of humanity lives on less than $10 a day.
- The poorest 40% of the world's population accounts for 5% of global income, while the richest 20% accounts for 75%.
- 22,000 children die each day due to poverty (UNICEF).
- Around 28% of all children in developing countries are estimated to be underweight or stunted. The two regions that account for the bulk of the deficit are South Asia and sub-Saharan Africa.
- An estimated 40 million people are living with HIV/AIDs, with three million deaths in 2004.
- Some 1.1 billion people in developing countries have inadequate access to water and 2.6 billion lack basic sanitation.[10]

As followers of Jesus become more aware of these needs, the desire to alleviate the suffering grows with it. And as biblical stewardship takes root—as we begin to see God's resources primarily to fulfill the agenda of the kingdom—we become a generous people, finding creative ways to give away our wealth (albeit wisely and carefully) such as "the graduated tithe" proposed by Ron Sider in his

---

[9]Tom Sine, *The New Conspirators*, 247.
[10]"Poverty Facts and Stats," *Global Issues*. http://www.globalissues.org/article/26/poverty-facts-and-stats> (accessed 24 November 2010).

classic *Rich Christians in an Age of Hunger*[11] or the aforementioned "Radical Experiment" being "conducted" in and through the people of the Church at Brook Hills in Birmingham. The Advent Conspiracy, a movement that seeks to save Christmas from the spirit of greed, over-consumption and over-commercialization, is yet another model that has helped many Christians and churches to truly celebrate Jesus during the holidays by genuinely reaching out to the poor and the lonely.[12] In one form or another, authentic biblical stewards live out a kingdom generosity, giving abundantly toward the alleviation of the suffering of their hungry, thirsty, naked and homeless neighbors around the world; for "how does God's love abide in anyone who has the world's goods and sees a brother or sister in need and yet refuses to help?" (1 John 3:17).

Commitment to the Simple Life

Kingdom generosity is authenticated by a commitment to the simple life, a third trait of biblical stewards. Something is not quite right when people claim to be generous (or viewed by the world as generous) and yet live luxuriously. Such generosity may be sincere, but it falls short of the biblical call to give sacrificially (Mark 12:41-44). Indeed to be truly generous is to ask at some point regarding our lifestyles, "How much is enough?"[13]

Contrary to the stereotype of those who decry extravagance and materialism, the call to simplicity does not just come from the radical, hippie, leftist fringe. For example, the Lausanne Covenant, a document that has served as the statement of faith and purpose for hundreds of evangelical churches and organizations around the world, states, "Those of us who live in affluent circumstances accept our duty to develop *a simple lifestyle* in order to contribute more generously to both relief and evangelism."[14] (Emphasis added)

---

[11] Ronald J. Sider, *Rich Christians in an Age of Hunger*, Fifth edition (W Publishing Group, 2005), 187-190.

[12] To find out more about the Advent Conspiracy, go to "Advent Conspiracy," http://www.advent conspiracy.org/ (accessed 24 November 2010).

[13] Platt, *Radical,* 107-140.

[14] "Lausanne Covenant," in John Stott, Ed. *Making Christ Known: Historic Mission Documents from the Lausanne Movement, 1974-1989* (Grand Rapids, MI: Eerdmans, 1996), 33-34.

Biblical stewards know, however, that the call to simplicity ultimately comes from Scripture. Biblical principles that build its case include the equalization of wealth as seen in the Year of Jubilee when God commanded all properties to be restored to their original owners (stewards?) and all debts to be cancelled (Lev. 25:8-38), the prophetic warnings against compassionless luxury (Amos 4:1-3; Jas. 5:1-8), and sacrificial concern for the poor as a prerequisite for discipleship (Luke 18:18-25).[15] Just like with kingdom generosity, the commitment to simplicity flows out of a biblically-grounded and heart-wrenching awareness that billions of people suffer from inadequate food supply, clean water, sturdy housing, security, and other realities of poverty. As the Lausanne Covenant states as the basis of the call to a simple lifestyle, "All of us are shocked by the poverty of millions and disturbed by the injustices which cause it."[16]

A commitment to simplicity embodies a number of key missional values. First, it reflects God's concern for the poor. By identifying with the poor by way of a simple lifestyle, we bear witness to the God of the poor. Second, it puts us in position to actually address human need by way of freed-up resources and freed-up time. Third, it frees us up to build community with one another. Rather than spending most of our time in the rat race in order to keep up with the Joneses, we free up space and time *from* the rat race in order to get to *know* the Joneses! And fourth, it challenges the idols of consumerism and materialism that so plague high society. Biblical stewards, who are committed to the simple life, bring gospel sanity to bear upon the out-of-control "lifestyles of the rich and famous" to which many people aspire.

The simple life looks differently from person to person and from church to church, so to sit in judgment against those who don't practice simplicity according to one's own rigid standards would violate the humility that accompanies simplicity. Popular American activist Shane Claiborne recalls a time when he flew to Toronto, Canada for a conference on simple living. Feeling pretty smug about how he and the rest of the folks at the Simple Way in Philadelphia were exemplifying the simple life, Claiborne ran into friend and then-editor of *Geez Magazine* Will Braun, who looked a little tired. When Claiborne

---

[15] For a more a just treatment of the biblical basis for simplicity, see Richard Foster, *Freedom of Simplicity* (San Francisco et al.: Harper & Row, 1981), 15-51.

[16] "Lausanne Covenant," 33.

inquired about it, he discovered that Braun, an advocate of the de-motorizing of society, had just arrived from bicycling a thousand miles to get to the conference![17] For some, the commitment to simple living might mean doing less driving and more carpooling; for others like Braun it might mean championing the de-motorization of society altogether. For some, simple living might mean downsizing to a smaller place; for others, it might mean living in intentional community.[18] For some, simple living might mean being mindful of their tendency to accumulate and thus buy less impulsively; for others, it might mean crusading against the proliferation of malls and the advertisement business, which preys upon the weaknesses and cravings of the populace.

Living out simplicity legalistically and judgmentally violates what Foster celebrates as "the freedom of simplicity." However, while there is an absolute need to resist prescribing the simple life for others, and thus, perpetuate a new kind of legalism,[19] biblical stewards are compelled to ask themselves and the church the following guiding question: "If we really care about the poor, how shall we then live?"

Creation Care

And fourthly, biblical stewards also demonstrate an acute appreciation for God's creation and therefore "walk gently on the earth."[20] The call to whole life stewardship necessarily extends to earth-keeping; perhaps it should even begin there, for the earth is what sustains all of life and the rest of God's good gifts. Relationships, property, possessions, money: none of these things means anything if we had no earth on which to enjoy them! But more than a mere stage on which the divine-human drama is played out, earth itself is part of the drama. God's smile upon completing creation in Gen. 1:25, thus

---

[17]Shane Claiborne in conversation with Tony Campolo, "Lifestyle" in *Simply Enough* DVD (Alternatives for Simple Living, 2007).

[18]See Sider, *Rich Christians*, 190-191. See also a short testimony of the Church of the Sojourners in San Francisco in Debbie Gish, "Creating a New Normal," *Conspire* 2/3 (Summer 2010), 48-49.

[19]Foster, *Freedom of Simplicity*, 112.

[20]This is the title of an excellent book on life choices that reflect genuine care for creation by Lisa Graham McMinn and Megan Anna Neff, *Walking Gently on the Earth* (Downers Grove, IL: IVP, 2010).

validating creation as valuable in and of itself apart from humankind, begins a steady stream of scripture that affirms creation's leading role in the divine-human drama.

The earth is also part of the drama (and not just a stage) in that God made humankind out of it (Gen. 2:7), thus establishing the organic interdependence between the earth and humanity in their relationship with the Creator. Indeed, God, humanity and the earth are in covenant community together.[21] Biblical stewards understand the integral connection between creation care and people care. "We are creatures of earth," explains sociologist Lisa Graham McMinn, "and so caring for earth is a way of caring for ourselves."[22]

This understanding of interdependence between the earth and people challenges the notion that earth-care has no place on the agenda of the church's mission. In the face of humanity's spiritual lostness and abject poverty, how can we justify spending even a single penny or a single minute on caring for trees and animals and the like? Besides, God has sanctioned humanity to have dominion over the earth, to subdue it. Such notions come from our tendency to dichotomize and see things as radically separate; as if the way in which we care or don't care about the created order does not have implications for the way in which we practice or not practice evangelism and our work among the poor. The truth is the church serves a God bent on saving creation and everyone in it. Indeed, the reconciliation of all things includes healing relationships between people and God, between people and people, and between God, people and creation (Rom. 8: 18-25). Biblical stewards affirm this interdependence and understand that "the whole mission" must include the care of creation.

What does creation care look like? Like with simple living, this is not the time for legalistic prescriptions and a judgmental spirit; but rather the time to keep ourselves accountable by asking tough, countercultural, anti-Global Dream questions. On a personal level, do I recycle? Do I minimize the use of disposal goods? Do I turn lights and electrical appliances off when they are not in use? How would our

---

[21] Zac Niringiye, "In the Garden of Eden I: Creation and Community," *Journal of Latin American Theology* 5/1 (2010): 18-31. In this insightful article, Niringiye makes a compelling case from the Bible's creation narratives for the harmony between God, creation, and humankind. All of the articles in this particular journal issue actually affirms this harmony and calls Christians to earth stewardship.

[22] McMinn and Neff, *Walking Gently*, 24.

homes fare in an environmental audit? On a more corporate level, do we care about issues such as climate change, global warming, deforestation, the mistreatment of animals, etc.? Do we support policies that promote the care of the environment? Biblical stewards ask themselves these kinds of questions and strive to "walk gently on the earth."

Preaching for Whole Life Stewardship

The following four summary principles can help guide missional preachers in forming a church full of whole-life stewards.

Kingdom Dream Vs. Global Dream

First, we preach an alternative definition of the good life and urge our members to pursue the Kingdom Dream over and against the Global Dream. "The journey towards whole-life discipleship," writes Sine, "begins when we struggle to translate the vision of God's better future into a whole new understanding of what the good life is all about."[23] Contrary to the stereotypical notion that to be Christian is to be out-of-touch with the real world and missing out on all the fun:

> God does not call us to a life of self-imposed misery and asceticism, any more than He calls us to a life of more successful scrambling. We are called to a life that is much more festive, celebrative, and satisfying than anything the rat race can offer. God calls us to a good life that elevates relationships, celebration, worship, family, community, and service above the values of acquisition, individualism, and materialism.[24]

As mentioned earlier, authentic biblical stewardship is not a popular subject precisely because it challenges what Sine calls the "the good life of the global mall."[25] It offends people; it angers us, because the preacher is meddling into a domain that we believe belongs solely

---

[23]Sine, *Why Settle for More*, 112.
[24]Ibid., 144.
[25]Sine, *New Conspirators*, 71ff.

to us. Furthermore, it makes us feel guilty for the lifestyles we live and the riches we enjoy; and heaven forbid if God's people start feeling guilty! If we preach whole life stewardship, members might leave and potential visitors might not visit. As such, church growth strategists would probably discourage us from preaching and teaching on it. It is true that missional preachers, who have been gripped by the vision of whole life stewardship, will not win any popularity contests anytime soon. But in light of the biblical truth of stewardship as set forth in this chapter, can we preach and teach anything less than the radical implications of the gospel upon our lives?

Relationships and Community: Investing in Human Resources

Second, we preach the priority of relationships, of community. Cultivating healthy relationships in family, church, and neighborhood is a stewardship issue in that we are investing in people, the greatest God-given resource. Many psychologists, sociologists and theologians alike have documented the consequences of the quest for "the good life," which include dehumanization, alienation, and loneliness, even if one makes it to the top of the heap.

What would happen if we measured wealth, not by our investments in finances and property, but by our investments in family, church, and neighborhood? We give mental assent to the notion that of all the earth's resources, human resources are the greatest, but I am not sure if we really believe it. What if we did? Missional preachers keep this question before the people, and with it lead them toward a greater, deeper experience of family, church, missional partnership, and human community.

Living with Global Poverty in View: Generosity and Simplicity

Third, we preach a lifestyle that has global poverty in view. Mark Labberton, President of Fuller Theological Seminary in Pasadena, CA, shares a practice he used to employ when serving the First Presbyterian Church in Berkeley, CA. He says in preparation for Sunday service, he would read the weekly update from a missionary family serving at-risk children in Cambodia. He would do this in order ". . . to be reminded of the realities of suffering in the world" and to lead Sunday morning worship accordingly.[26] Such a practice can only lead to "dangerous worship" that cultivates an awareness of unimaginable poverty experienced by billions of people around the planet.

We preach lifestyles that reflect this awareness—namely, lifestyles of kingdom generosity and a commitment to the simple life. We preach sacrificial giving (where the tithe is only the beginning), such as what Platt urges his church as part of the Radical Experiment: "For one year," he pleads, "sacrifice your money—every possible dollar—in order to spend your life radically on specific, urgent spiritual and physical need in the world."[27] We preach not just sacrifice, but the joy of sacrifice. It *is* better to give than to receive! From the perspective of the Global Dream, this adage does not make sense at all; but through the eyes of the Kingdom Dream, "those who lose their life for [Jesus'] sake will find it" (Matt. 8:39).

We preach against materialism, consumerism and the rat race and preach the rewards of the simple life—the rewards of freedom from the power of mammon, as well as the freedom to give more time to cultivate relationships and engage in God's mission. Missional preachers preach "the freedom of simplicity." Coupled with kingdom generosity, preaching the simple life equips God's people to take part in God's transforming work among the lost and the poor of the world.

Living with Creation in View

And lastly, we preach a lifestyle that has God's creation in view. We preach against the utilitarian view of creation. In this view, "God's good creation is seen as nothing more than provision of the resources needed to achieve [the Global] Dream."[28] Over and against this view, we preach a biblical steward's view of creation, in which humanity is but a part—albeit a special part—of a greater ecological system created and set in motion by the God of the universe. The part that humanity plays is exactly that of stewarding the earth and everything in it. We preach being responsible with all that God has given us, including most fundamentally the earth that sustains us, and thus lead the redeemed in

---

[26]Mark Labberton, *The Dangerous Act of Worship: Living God's Call to Justice* (Downers Grove, IL: IVP, 2007), 33-34.
[27]Platt, *Radical,* 196.
[28]Sine, *New Conspirators,* 80.

Christ into a harmonious relationship with God, each other, and the environment.

Missional preachers preach whole life stewardship, where perspectives on wealth align with the kingdom, where relationships and community are priority, where generosity and simplicity define our lives for the sake of the poor, and where our relationship with the earth becomes a part of our understanding of God's mission in the world. As we preach in this way week-in and week-out, God's call upon humanity in general and the church in particular to be whole life stewards for the sake of the redemption of creation and everyone in it will be heard clearly by all.

Preaching for *Shalom:* Life and Peace[1]

Al Tizon

Abortion-on-demand, drugs, war, and gun violence—issues against which this author has fought as an activist through the years—have something in common: they diminish and destroy life. The driving conviction for many activists is the sacredness of life and the ethical call to resist the violence that seeks to destroy it.

To fight against violence and destruction—or more positively, to protect life and to work toward peace—seems agreeable enough to all. After all, "only psychopaths and sociopaths can without remorse destroy the lives of others,"[2] and "No sane human being would say that war and conflict are preferable to peace."[3] And yet, just from the short list above, good Christian people find themselves on the opposite sides of each of those issues. Many of those who fight against abortion, for example, are conservative evangelicals, who view protesting government-sponsored war as unpatriotic. And many of those who denounce war are political and theological progressives who see a woman's right to choose as paramount over the life of her unborn child. A proper view of the kingdom of God, however, sees the inconsistency within both conservative and progressive positions.

---

[1] Adapted from *Missional Preaching: Engage, Embrace, Transform* by Al Tizon, copyright © 2012 by Judson Press. Used by permission of Judson Press. It was also one of the lectures given at the 2015 William Menzies Lectureship, Asia Pacific Theological Seminary in Baguio City, Philippines.

[2] Lowell O. Erdahl, *Pro-Life/Pro-Peace: Life Affirming Alternatives to Abortion, War, Mercy-Killing and the Death Penalty* (Minneapolis: Augsburg, 1986), 14.

[3] Cynthia Wedel, "Is Peace Controversial," in *Preaching on Peace,* eds. Ronald J. Sider and Darrel J. Brubaker (Philadelphia: Fortress, 1982): 18.

Shalom (Life and Peace) in a Violent World

Abortion and war—the issues most people associate with life and peace respectively—are extremely sensitive; as such, to make a case for the relationship between life and peace can potentially offend just about everyone! The life-peace connection, however, can serve as a bridge across the conservative-progressive divide; for the gospel of life and the gospel of peace are the same gospel. We are called to be both "pro-life" and "pro-peace" in the most authentic sense of these terms. These "pro-" terms are hopelessly loaded in the Western nations, as political activists have co-opted them for their own ends. However, in Asia, these terms are not impacted by political ideologies and thus have the ability to create a bridge between those who protect life and those who make peace.

Several Christian social activists-theologians in the 1980s and 90s, such as the late Cardinal Joseph Bernardin and Ronald J. Sider, did significant "bridge work" across party lines by employing terms such as *consistent life ethic*,[4] *completely pro-life*,[5] and *the seamless garment*,[6] thus creating language for people who desire to live and vote according to the higher laws of life and peace.

Whatever terminology is used for this bridge work, it refers to "a moral commitment to respecting, protecting, and enhancing human life at every stage and in every context."[7] The purpose statement of the organization appropriately called "Consistent Life: Voices for Peace and Life" provides a practical angle to the definition, by stating, "We serve the anti-violence community by connecting issues, building bridges, and strengthening the case against each kind of socially-approved killing by consistently opposing them all."[8]

---

[4] Joseph L. Bernardin, "A Consistent Ethic of Life," in *Seamless Garment*, ed. Thomas A. Nairn (Maryknoll, NY: Orbis, 2008), 7–20.

[5] Ronald J. Sider, *Completely Pro-Life* (Downers Grove: IVP, 1986).

[6] Even though the term has been attributed to Bishop Joseph L. Bernardin, it was actually coined by Eileen Egan, a member of the Catholic Worker and peace activist, in a 1971 interview. See M. Therese Lysaught, "From the Challenge of Peace to the Gift of Peace," in *The Consistent Ethic of Life*, ed. Thomas A. Nairn (Maryknoll, NY: Orbis, 2008), 112–13.

[7] David Gushee, "The Consistent Ethic of Life," *Christian Ethics Today: Journal of Christian Ethics* 7/1 (February 2000).

[8] Consistent Life Homepage, www.consistent-life.org/index.html (accessed 3 December 2010).

As terms go, the word *shalom* conveys the consistency between life and peace in a concise way, as it captures the biblical vision of wholeness. Translated most often in the English as "peace," it can also be defined as "the fullness of life."[9] *Shalom* is what results when God reigns as Redeemer and Lord. Life and peace characterize *shalom* existence. As the National Council of Catholic Bishops' "Challenge of Peace" statement says, "No society can live in peace with itself, or with the world, without a full awareness of the worth and dignity of every human person."[10]

The fundamental enemy of life and peace is death-dealing violence, which manifests on every level of human existence, from world wars to hatred in the human heart, and everything in between. According to the biblical story, humanity's propensity toward violence is a consequence of the Fall in Genesis 3. Indeed, the first murder is recorded in the very next chapter when Cain killed Abel (Gen. 4:8-10). According to Walter Wink, "The Fall affirms the radicality of evil."[11] And this evil includes humanity's bent toward violence. Wink goes on to say that the Fall points to a deeper reality of the human condition— "a layer of sludge beneath the murky waters that can be characterized only as a hellish hatred of the light, of truth, of kindness and compassion, *a brute lust for annihilation*" (emphasis added).[12] From bullying to domestic abuse, from homicide to genocide, from terrorism to torture, we live in a dangerously violent world.[13] The gospel of the kingdom counteracts this violence by offering "the third way" of Jesus, which essentially refers to the way of nonviolent engagement.[14]

---

[9] Sider, *Completely Pro-Life*, 11–31 (see esp. 15–16).

[10] Quoted in Lysaught, "From the Challenge of Peace to the Gift of Peace," 114.

[11] Walter Wink, *Engaging the Powers: Discernment and Resistance in a World of Domination* (Minneapolis: Fortress, 1992), 69.

[12] Wink, *Engaging*, 69.

[13] I would include in this list the violence to the unborn. For many, however, I recognize the violence of abortion is not readily apparent. To those who are interested in learning more about such violence, see "Types of Abortion Procedures," American Pregnancy Association. www.americanpregnancy.org/unplannedpregnancy/abortionprocedures.html (accessed December 3, 2010).

[14] Wink, *Engaging*, 175–93.

Cultivating *Shalom,* a Culture of Life and Peace

Peace activists Alan Kreider, Eleanor Kreider, and Paulus Widjaja make a biblical case for the church to become "a culture of peace . . . in which unreconciled enemies are reconciled . . . unforgiven people are forgiven and . . . they are given a common mission—to share the 'good news of peace' with all nations."[15] And given the connection between life and peace, it makes sense to extend it to "a culture of life and peace," i.e., a culture of *shalom*. What are some characteristics of Christians and churches that are being cultivated in the fertile soil of *shalom*?

Respect for Life at Every Stage

The groundwork for this characteristic has already been laid, but a brief expansion of it here locates it among the core elements of a *shalom* person and a *shalom* church. To ones who have been restored in Christ to a right relationship with God, the Creator and Giver of Life, life takes on intrinsic value. Lutheran bishop Lowell Erdahl points out, "While Christianity has no monopoly on reverence for life, it is a central Christian affirmation."[16] Biblical faith teaches that life has intrinsic value because God created it (Gen. 1-2). Furthermore, human life carries particular value because humans were created in God's own image (Gen. 1:26-27). Zac Niringiye notes, "Whereas the other creatures are made 'according to their kinds,' humanity is made 'in [God's] image, in [God's] likeness.'"[17] As such, although all life warrants our respect, human life deserves our deepest and highest respect.

As if it is not enough to value life simply because God created it, we should also consider the truth that "For God so loved the world that he gave his only Son, so that everyone who believes in him may not perish but may have eternal life" (John 3:16). "It is crucial to see," asserts Ron Sider, "that the biblical teaching about eternal life does not

---

[15]Alan Kreider, Eleanor Kreider, and Paulus Widjaja, *A Culture of Peace* (Intercourse, PA: Good Books, 2005), 16–17.
[16]Erdahl, *Pro-Life/Pro-Peace*, 14.
[17]Zac Niringiye, "In the Garden of Eden – I," *Journal of Latin American Theology* 5/1 (2010): 26.

refer to some ethereal, spiritual fairyland totally unrelated to human history and the created order."[18] In other words, the idea of eternal life is not limited to a future bliss but also to abundant life now (John 10:10). Apparently, God deemed the world valuable enough to heal, and every human life as valuable enough to save in Jesus Christ. Furthermore, asserts Baptist ethicist David Gushee:

> Every life means every life, without exception. That includes two-month-along developing human beings in the womb, poor babies in Bangladesh, impoverished children in ghettos, abused wives and children, civilians in war zones, wounded soldiers at Walter Reed, imprisoned detainees in the war on terror, aging people in nursing homes, mentally handicapped people, people convicted of heinous crimes. Everyone.[19]

Based upon the life-giving doctrines of creation and redemption, a person's worth is not based upon his or her age, physical or mental condition, socioeconomic status, or usefulness in society. As Christians, we need no other reason to affirm the value of human life than the fact that each and every human being is made in the image of God and is profoundly loved by God. To do violence to the living therefore—to harm, injure, kill—is wrong. "Thou shall not kill" (Ex. 20:13).

One of the most powerful and beautiful truths about the death and resurrection of Christ is that the final enemy of death has been defeated (1 Cor. 15:54-57). Through Jesus' ministry of life-giving words, liberating deeds, atoning death, and resurrection power, life—and not death—has become the final word for all time. As a result, in the power of the Spirit, followers of Jesus—*shalom* people—challenge death and all its ways, resisting unthinking absolutism and respecting life at every stage from womb to tomb.

We need to be prayerfully sensitive to extreme cases in which the tragic choice to end a life may be permissible, such as when one life is endangered by another. However, societies go tragically awry when

---

[18]Sider, *Completely Pro-Life*, 18.
[19]David Gushee, "Opinion: Retrieving a Consistent Pro-Life Ethic," *Associated Baptist Press* (7 March 2007) www.abpnews.com/content/view/1950/120/ (accessed 12 December 2010).

they make exceptions to the law of the land, such as abortion-on-demand, capital punishment, and preemptive war.[20] More could be said about these types of exceptions; but rather than focus on them, the emphasis here is the normative rule for *shalom* people—namely, to respect, defend, and protect life, from the unborn to the elderly and everyone in between who are threatened by the death-dealing violence of this world.

Human Flourishing

But *shalom* is not satisfied with merely the defense and protection of life; it seeks the fullness of life. Another way of putting it is that *shalom* people are ultimately not "anti-" people but "pro-" people. We are truly "pro-life" in the sense that we participate in activities and institutions that cultivate human flourishing. Although human flourishing is a largely philosophical term that has synonyms such as *happiness, self-actualization, empowerment,* or *transformation,* I believe the term is especially effective in conveying the *shalom* image of human beings blossoming to their full potential in harmony with God, one another, and the rest of creation. An InterVarsity Christian Fellowship document introducing a conference on human flourishing states, "We are called to nurture life within ourselves, our communities, and in our world. Abundant life is a quality of the kingdom of God and from this root grows our commitment to human flourishing."[21] Being truly *for* life and not just *against* death, *shalom* Christians seek to enable all persons, from conception to old age, to flourish in the name of Jesus Christ and by the power of the Spirit.

Practically, this commitment to human flourishing means helping broken, vulnerable people—those diminished by poverty, oppression, and conflict—move toward wholeness. In the words of theologian Vinay Samuel, "[The poor] need their personhood . . . restored."[22] Samuel goes on to elaborate on ten dimensions of personhood, which include the physical, psycho-emotional, social, ethical, and spiritual

---

[20]Erdahl, *Pro-Life/Pro-Peace,* 24-28.
[21]"Human Flourishing—A Thematic Overview," InterVarsity www.intervarsity.org/gfm/download.php?id= 6649&version_id=9219 (accessed December 10, 2010).
[22]Vinay Samuel, "Mission as Transformation," *Transformation* 19/4 (October 2002): 244.

areas of the human person that need restoration and development.[23] For those who are against abortion, for example, a commitment to human flourishing should manifest in activities such as finding adoptive homes for children, taking in foster children, and supporting ministries to assist young, single mothers. And for those who protest gun violence and war, a commitment to human flourishing should be expressed in activities such as caring for veterans, grieving with families who have lost loved ones to war, and participating in reconciliation work between warring factions.

Our mission toward human flourishing—our proactive striving to help fellow human beings reach their God-envisioned potential (even as we strive to do this ourselves)—is the necessary affirmative aspect of our commitment to *shalom*, which "calls us to reverence life, to support everything that enhances and ennobles life and to oppose everything that degrades and destroys life."[24]

The Way of Nonviolence

The way of nonviolent engagement constitutes a third characteristic of *shalom* people. We take seriously the teachings of the Master to love our enemies (Matt. 5:43-48) and to put away the sword (Matt. 26:42), and we interpret Jesus' death on the cross as his way of overcoming hate with love and evil with good (Matt. 26:53; Rom. 12:17-21). We see neither retaliation nor passivity as acceptable responses to the world's death-dealing violence; we see a third way.

Popularized by New Testament scholar Walter Wink, this "third way" is the radical way of nonviolent resistance, based primarily upon the teachings of Jesus concerning turning the other check, giving one's undergarment, and going the second mile (Matt. 5:38-42; Luke 6:29-30). Contrary to popular interpretations that these illustrations teach victims to subject themselves to further humiliation and pain in response to bully tactics, Wink shows that they actually convey resistance by denying a bully the power to humiliate while simultaneously seizing the moral initiative in the situation. For

---

[23]Samuel, "Mission as Transformation," 245–46. See also Al Tizon, *Transformation After Lausanne* (Oxford, et al: Regnum; Eugene, OR: Wipf & Stock, 2008), 145–147, where I go into more detail in interpreting Samuel's concept of personhood.

[24]Erdahl, *Pro-Life/Pro-Peace,* 19.

example, in Jesus' time and culture, "turning the other cheek" would force an offender to strike the victim on the left cheek, which was willfully offered. But this action actually elevates the victim to equal social status—the exact opposite of what the striker intended. Nonviolent resistance disarms the violator while maintaining the dignity of the victim. According to Wink, this and the other two illustrations demonstrated a third way of response to dominant violators of human dignity and life—not the first way of violent retaliation nor the second way of cowering acquiescence, but the third way of nonviolent, righteous resistance.[25] Wink cautions, however, that we must be responsible in teaching nonviolence to victims of domestic abuse, racism, and the like, lest we teach them the way of passivity and cowardice.[26]

In order for nonviolent righteous resistance to be useful, it must be operationalized. Peace activist Richard K. Taylor offers five principles that can help guide *shalom* Christians in the way of gospel nonviolence:[27]

1. A deep faith in God and God's power (Rom. 1:16; 2 Thess. 1:11). Gospel nonviolence is so contrary to fallen human nature that it takes nothing less than deep faith to enable us to practice it—even for Jesus (see Matt. 26:39).
2. A resolve to resist injustice—or, stated more positively, a strong sense of justice (Jer. 7:5-7; Mic. 6:8).
3. Goodwill toward wrongdoers (Luke 6:35-36; Rom. 12:14-21).
4. A willingness to suffer for what is right (Matt. 5:10-12; 1 Pet. 2:19-21).
5. A refusal to inflict suffering on others (Zech. 7:9-10; Matt. 22:39).

If these guiding principles seem superhuman, it is because they are; go back to Principle 1!

---

[25]Wink, *Engaging*, 175–86. I have hardly touched the surface of Wink's brilliant exegesis of these passages. For its full impact, one must read Wink's book, especially the pages listed here.
[26]Ibid., 189–93.
[27]Richard K. Taylor, *Love in Action: A Direct Action Handbook for Catholics Using Gospel Nonviolence to Reform and Renew the Church* (Philadelphia: R.K. Taylor, 2007), 16–20.

Waging Peace

Finally, *shalom* Christians understand the proactive aspect of peace—namely, the call to make peace, to initiate it and help shape the world by it. It is not enough to keep the peace or to respond nonviolently to enemies of peace; we must also advance to make peace. Jesus said, "Blessed are the peace*makers,* for they will be called children of God" (Matt. 5:9).

To wage peace takes on at least three practical dimensions. First, *shalom* Christians forgive, as they bask in God's forgiveness for them (Matt. 6:14-15). A church cannot promote peace in the world unless it learns to extend forgiveness even to those who have done great harm. The story of Eric Irivuzumugabe comes to mind. A Tutsi who survived the infamous Rwandan genocide, Irivuzumugabe learned to forgive the Hutus, who massacred many of his loved ones and friends.[28] The story of the Amish community that extended forgiveness to the man who murdered five of their children and injured five others in a school shooting in Nickel Mines, Pennsylvania, also comes to mind.[29] These stories speak of "the divine logic of forgiveness."[30] To forgive is to wage peace.

Second, inseparably related to forgiveness is the practice of reconciliation. We are commanded not just to love our neighbors but also to love our enemies. The ministry of reconciliation ensures that forgiveness goes the distance (Rom. 5:18-20). In a sermon on loving our enemies, Martin Luther King Jr. preached, "We can never say, 'I will forgive you, but I won't have anything further to do with you.' Forgiveness means reconciliation, a coming together again. Without this, no man can love his enemies."[31]

And third, *shalom* Christians engage in subversive acts of compassion and justice. By "subversive," I mean to emphasize that we aid those suffering due to political conflict or injustice, not just because

---

[28] Eric Irivuzumugabe, *My Father, Maker of the Trees: How I Survived the Rwandan Genocide* (Grand Rapids: Baker, 2009). For a short article adapted from the book, see "Seventy Times Seven," *Prism* 17/1 (Jan/Feb 2010), 9–11.

[29] This story can be found in Donald Kraybill, Steven Nolt, and David Weaver-Zercher, *Amish Grace* (San Francisco: Jossey-Bass, 2010).

[30] Kristyn Komarnicki, "The Divine Logic of Forgiveness," *Prism* 17/1 (January/February 2010): 2.

[31] Martin Luther King Jr. *Strength to Love* (New York: Pocket Books, 1968), 43.

they need desperate help, but also as a statement to the powers that their decisions destroy lives. To wage peace is to oppose war and injustice by helping the suffering poor who are so often caught in the crossfire.

Preaching for *Shalom*

The following three guidelines can help missional preachers who aim to cultivate *shalom* in their congregations.

Consistent Ethic of Life and Peace

We preach a commitment to life because we are committed to peace, and we preach a commitment to peace because we are committed to life. We see the relational consistency between them in the kingdom of God, so we preach life and peace together. "To set the mind on the flesh is death," penned the apostle Paul, "but to set the mind on the Spirit is life and peace" (Rom. 8:6). We preach this consistent ethic despite pressure to conform to a particular political ideology. As both conservatives and liberals draw their lines in the sand, it becomes increasingly more difficult for people to challenge any part of the respective agendas of the right or the left. "The power of [political] Party identity is so profound," writes Gushee, "that otherwise thoughtful people lose the capacity for independent reflection."[32]

God forbid that conservatives question American-declared war or help in the work of gun violence prevention, and God forbid that progressives join in the fight against abortion-on-demand or speak out against the dehumanization of women through pornography. Gushee speaks for himself, but captures the conviction needed for missional preaching, when he declares, "As a Christian, I believe that no force is to be allowed to compete with God's word for the government of my life in any aspect. This includes Party loyalty."[33] Preaching for *shalom* does not cater to left or right ideologies; we preach the kingdom God, which respects and promotes life from womb to tomb, consistently and courageously.

---

[32]Gushee, "Opinion."
[33]Ibid.

Forgiveness and Reconciliation

We preach forgiveness and reconciliation, which are fundamental to the good news of Christ. They are fundamental in the sense that the Christian faith rests completely on the God who has seen fit to forgive and reconcile. In response, we extend forgiveness and reconciliation to others. The parable of the wicked slave in Matthew 18 forcefully illustrates this. We know the story: In his mercy, the king forgave a slave of all his debt. But later on, that same slave found another slave who owed him money; and when the second slave could not pay, the first slave had him thrown in jail. When the king found out, he told the one he had forgiven, "You wicked slave! I forgave you all that debt because you pleaded with me. Should you not have had mercy on your fellow slave, as I had mercy on you?" The king then had him imprisoned until he paid his whole debt (Matt. 18:21-35).

Kreider and colleagues note, "God's command to his people is not simply to accept his forgiveness; it is to act forgivingly to other people. It is not simply to be reconciled to God; it is to be reconciled to other people."[34] Preaching for *shalom* calls God's people to forgive others as our heavenly Father has forgiven us (Matt. 6:14-15; 18:21-35), and it calls us to seek reconciliation wherever conflict and brokenness reside, just as God has reached out to be reconciled to us (2 Cor. 5:18-20).

Peacemaking unto Death

We preach sacrificial peacemaking. We preach that "a harvest of righteousness is sown in peace for those who make peace" (Jas 3:18). As the late Vernon C. Grounds once preached, "The God of peace . . . summons us, as disciples of Jesus Christ, to be peacemakers in our marriages, our homes, our friendships, our neighborhoods, our churches, our places of business and work, our country, and our world."[35] Making peace in a world bent on violence and death is not easy; in fact, it is impossible without the resources available to us in the Spirit. In the same sermon, Grounds told his audience that, "God has

---

[34] Kreider, Kreider, and Widjaja, *Culture of Peace*, 111.
[35] Vernon C. Grounds, "Spiritual Weapons for Waging Peace," in *Preaching on Peace,* eds. Ronald J. Sider and Darrel J. Brubaker (Philadelphia: Fortress, 1982), 62.

put at our disposal effective weapons for the waging of peace."³⁶ He went on to say that the Christian's ultimate weapon is prayer—"a weapon infinitely more powerful than all the guns and bayonets, tanks and planes, battleships and bombs of all the nations in all the world."³⁷

In addition to urging God's people to pray for peace, preaching for *shalom* denounces acts of violence, from domestic abuse to homicide to genocide to war. Some issues are clearer than others. Torture, for example, has no place in the gospel and therefore preachers should have no qualms denouncing such a practice from the pulpit, even if it implicates one's own government. The same can be said of the genocide of whole peoples in places like Darfur in the Sudan. The long term violence between the Philippine government and the Muslims on the island of Mindanao is another case in point—as Aldrin Peñamora details for us elsewhere in this issue. These types of atrocities require prophetic preaching that openly confronts despotic governments, as well as inspires the church to engage in ministries of compassion, justice, and advocacy.

This type of preaching is dangerous as it inspires the redeemed in Christ to risk their lives; for often, the powers turn on peacemakers. This is the "sacrificial" part of peacemaking. For example, Christian Peacemaker Teams (CPT), an organization that applies "the same discipline and self-sacrifice to nonviolent peacemaking that armies devote to war," forms teams that "seek to follow God's Spirit as they work through local peacemakers who risk injury and death by waging nonviolent direct action to confront systems of violence and oppression."³⁸ The story of Tom Fox exemplifies the ultimate sacrifice of peacemaking. A CPT member working in Baghdad, Fox was abducted in November 2005 along with three other CPTers. While the other three were released after four months in captivity, Fox was not; he was shot dead and his body found on March 9, 2006.³⁹ Preaching for *shalom* aims to strengthen the church's commitment to peacemaking in a violent world no matter the cost. In light of the cross, which our Lord

---

³⁶Ibid., 63.
³⁷Ibid., 64.
³⁸"Mission Statement," *Christian Peacemaker Teams,* www.cpt.org/about/mission (accessed December 13, 2010).
³⁹"U.S. Hostage in Iraq Confirmed Dead," *BBC News* (March 11, 2006) http://news.bbc.co.uk/2/hi/ middle_east/4795678.stm (accessed December 13, 2010).

endured in order to show another way—a third way—can we preach anything less?

The grand biblical vision of *shalom* captivates missional preachers, and as such, we preach a consistent ethic of life and peace, we preach forgiveness and reconciliation, and we preach radical peace-making. We do this in the context of rival messages of violence, retribution, terrorism, and death. "The great challenge of Christians," ethicist David Gil says, "is to move out into the world and into our neighborhoods with another message and another agenda—that of our Lord of Life and Prince of Peace."[40]

---

[40]David Gil, *Doing Right: Practicing Ethical Principles* (Downers Grove: IVP, 2004), 215.

Eucharistic Justice: A Christ-Centered Response to the Bangsamoro Question in the Philippines

by Aldrin M. Peñamora

Introduction

Presently, House Bill No. 4994, known as the Bangsamoro Basic Law, is in the hands of the Philippine Congress. This bill is the culmination of several years of negotiations between the Philippine government and the Moro Islamic Liberation Front (MILF)—negotiations that have the primary purpose of securing lasting peace for the *Bangsa Moro* (Moro Nation) of Mindanao. Indeed, from the time of that Spanish conquistadores (with their swords and the Christian cross) landed on Philippine shores almost five centuries ago, peace has eluded the Muslims of Mindanao. Sadly, the Spanish colonizers introduced a type of Christianity via "massive military and religious campaigns to subdue local armed resistance and stamp out indigenous religious beliefs and practices."[1] It is thus said of the Muslim sons and daughters of Mindanao that, from the mid-16th century up to the very present, "There is no Moro generation that has not fought or witnessed war in their homeland."[2] As a consequence of struggling against often vastly superior forces, the Muslims of the Philippines who previously had

---

[1] O. D. Corpuz, *The Roots of the Filipino Nation*, vol. 1 (Quezon City, Philippines: AKLAHI, 1989), 46, cited in Abraham Iribani, *Give Peace a Chance: The Story of the GRP-MNLF Peace Talks* (Mandaluyong City, Philippines: Magbassa Kita, 2006), 17.

[2] Parouk S. Hussin, "Challenge of War and Search for Peace" in Amina Rasul, ed., *The Road to Peace and Reconciliation: Muslim Perspective on the Mindanao Conflict* (Makati City, Philippines: AIM, 2003), 11. The term "Moro" is used interchangeably in the Philippines with the term Muslim or, more specifically, with those Muslims who mostly inhabit islands in Mindanao. It is a Spanish term for the word Moor, which refers to the Muslim people of mixed Arab and Berber descent who occupied Spain in the 8th century. However, the epithet "Moro" as used by the early Spanish colonizers was anchored on their two observations: first, the Moros were savages bent only on plunder as guided by their "false" Islamic religion; second, their savage nature can only be rectified by subjugating them and civilizing them through Christianization. Samuel K. Tan, "Filipino Muslim Perceptions of Their History and Culture as Seen Through Indigenous Written Sources" in U.P. Center for Integrative and Development Studies, *Memories, Visions, Scholarship, and Other Essays* (Quezon City, Philippines: UP, 2001), 93.

dominion over those islands have now become an impoverished minority in their own homeland.[3]

With its significant natural resources and rich historical, social, and cultural heritage, Mindanao has fittingly been called "The Land of Promise." Alas, due to the persistence of violent conflicts, the Moros Mindanao has become a land of unfulfilled promises and broken dreams. Thus, the quest for peace cannot and must not be severed from the quest for justice. Filipino Muslim scholar Salah Jubair says correctly that, "Peace requires not only the absence of violence, but also the presence of justice." Moreover, he says, "If there is going to be a healing process, it must begin and end in justice."[4]

Such narrative, nonetheless, seems to have been lost from Filipino Christians' memories. But as Christianity is founded upon the veracity of our faith community's memory,[5] it is essential that Filipino Christians remember the events that have been instrumental in shaping Christianity in the Philippines. One such event has been our dealings with the Bangsamoro people.

In this paper, I am addressing the issue of justice, more specifically, economic justice for the Bangsamoro through a theological-ethical lens. Whereas other approaches reject the resources offered by faith traditions, I believe, as John H. Yoder remarked, that the renewal to which the whole world is called to confess cannot be made independently from the witness of the church community, but, rather, such confession is derived from the church's witness.[6] It is in this regard that the central practice of the Lord's Supper, or Eucharist, is relevant. I contend that, far from being a socially abstract ritual, the Eucharist is a crucial resource for a Christian justice and peacemaking

---

[3]Al-Gazel Rasul, ed., *Still Chasing the Rainbow: Selected Writings of Jainal D. Rasul, Sr. on Filipino Muslims' Politics, History, and Law (Shari'ah)* (Quezon City, Philippines: FedPil, 1999), 6.

[4]Salah Jubair, *The Long Road to Peace: Inside the GRP-MILF Peace Process* (Davao City, Philippines: Institute of Bangsamoro Studies, 2007), 7, 9. See also Mark Turner, "Resolving Self-Determination Disputes Through Complex Power-Sharing Arrangements: The Case of Mindanao, Southern Philippines," in *Settling Self-Determination Disputes: Complex Power-Sharing in Theory and Practice*, ed. Mark Weller and Barbara Metzger (Leiden, Netherlands: Brill, 2008), 192. Turner writes: "Such a peace does not simply mean a cessation of armed hostilities but also entails mutual respect for culture, religion, and locality, the feeling of security in daily lives, the expectation of decent services and ecologically sound development, human dignity, and the capacity to earn a living. When these things are achieved, there will be peace in Mindanao."

[5]Eduardo Hoornaert, *The Memory of the Christian People* (Maryknoll, NY: Orbis, 1988), 3-4.

[6]John H. Yoder, *Body Politics: Five Practices of the Christian Community Before the Watching World* (Scottsdale, Arizona: Herald, 1992), 78.

ethic that bids us to alleviate injustice and to advance the well-being of the oppressed, such as the Bangsamoro people. As Paul Bernier says, in the Eucharist, "We were not challenged simply to repeat his words, or institute a ritual action; we were asked to do as he did, to offer our lives that others might live."[7]

The "Moro Problem:" A Question of Injustice

The Moro Problem refers to the "historical and systematic marginalization and minorization of the . . . Moros, in their own homeland in the Mindanao islands, first by colonial powers from Spain . . . then the United States . . . and more recently by successor Philippine governments dominated by an elite with a Christian-Western orientation."[8] While there are several interconnected issues that comprise the Moro Problem (e.g., economic destitution, political marginalization, preservation of Moro identity, religious intolerance), according to the World Bank, which in 2005 performed a Joints Needs Assessment in Mindanao, such issues can be dovetailed into a single root cause—injustice,[9] that is, injustice committed by a largely Christian nation through its governments on a community that it has not sufficiently understood. As Robert McAmis perceptively remarks, the Moro Problem is "primarily the problem of not understanding the Muslim."[10] *The so-called Moro Problem, when examined open-mindedly, is really about the Christians being the problem of the Moros.* (Emphasis mine)

---

[7]Paul Bernier, *Broken Bread and Shared: Broadening Our Vision of the Eucharist* (Notre Dame, IN: Ave Maria, 1981), 86.

[8]Soliman Santos, Jr., "Evolution of the Armed Conflict on the Moro Front," A Background Paper Submitted for the Philippine Human Development Report 2005. Available from http://hdn.org.ph/wp-content/uploads/2005_PHDR/2005%20Evolution_Moro_Conflict.pdf (accessed 11 January 2014). The classic definition of the Moro Problem was given by Najeeb M. Saleeby in *The Moro Problem: An Academic Discussion of the History and Solution of the Problem of the Government of the Moros of the Philippine Island* (Manila, Philippines: E. C. McCullough, 1913), 16. He writes, "By the Moro problem is meant that method or form of administration by which the Moros and other non-Christians who are living among them, can be governed to their best interest and welfare in the most peaceful way possible, and can at the same time be provided with appropriate measures for their gradual advancement in culture and civilization, so that in the course of a reasonable time they can be admitted into the general government of the Philippine Islands as qualified members. . . . "

[9]Salah Jubair, *The Long Road to Peace: Inside the GRP-MILF Peace Process*, 5-6, citing World Bank Report on Mindanao Joint Needs Assessment Reconstruction and Development Program in a meeting with leaders of the MILF on March 12, 2005, Cotabato City, Philippines.

[10]Robert McAmis, "Muslim Filipinos: 1970-1972," *Mindanao Journal* III, nos. 3-4 (January-June 1977): 56.

As I mentioned, while the spreading of Catholicism was a key impetus in the Spanish conquest of the Philippines, the economic exploitation of the country was an equally important motivation. Jubair makes this pointed remark: "Spain came to the Philippines not so much for the Cross . . . religion was merely used to justify what otherwise was a satanic lust for worldly gain and glory."[11] Now, key to the Moro's economic destitution is their *ancestral land*, the best parts from which they were driven out as ownership was handed over to Christian Filipinos and foreign-owned corporations. Such policy fundamentally goes against the Moro Islamic belief about property, which upholds that ancestral domain is *waqaf*, or property in trust. Thus, to lose their ancestral domain was debilitating for the Moros, for their social existence directly revolves around those lands.[12] Whereas the Moros had owned most of the land in Mindanao on the eve of American colonization at the turn of the 20th century, by 1981 the Bangsamoro owned less than seventeen percent, most of which was located in remote and barren areas.[13] So central is this issue that the success or failure of peace negotiations hinges on its resolution; indeed, the Bangsamoro's claim to the rights to their ancestral lands must be understood as "the core of the expression of their right to self determination."[14]

Further aggravating Moro poverty is the fact that most development efforts by the Philippine government, which is usually composed of a Christian majority, have been directed to improve primarily the conditions of Christian settlers. Studies done in 1970 showed that regions inhabited by Moros were among those with the highest infant mortality and unemployment rates; they also had the fewest doctors to provide health services and lagged far behind in terms of educational services and other necessities, such as water and power systems.[15] Reports in 2006 and 2009 invariably demonstrated how

---

[11]Salah Jubair, *A Nation Under Endless Tyranny*, 3rd ed. (Kuala Lumpur, Malaysia: IQ Marin, 1999), 54.

[12]Lualhati Abreu, "Ancestral Domain—the Core Issue," in *The Moro Reader: History and the Contemporary Struggles of the Bangsamoro People*, ed. Bobby M. Tuazon (Quezon City, Philippines: CenPEG, 2008), 51.

[13]Aijaz Ahmad, "Class and Colony in Mindanao," in *Rebels, Warlords and Ulama*, ed. Eric Gutierrez et al. (Quezon City: Institute for Popular Democracy, 1999), 13. See also Internal Displacement Monitoring Centre (IDMC) and the Norwegian Refugee Council (NRC), "Cycle of Conflict and Neglect: Mindanao's Displacement and Protection Crisis," October 2009, 4; available from www.internal-displacement.org (accessed 31 January 2014).

[14]Myrthena L. Fianza, "Indigenous Patterns of Land Ownership," *Mindanao Focus*; quoted in Abreu, "Ancestral Domain," 48.

[15]Macapado Abaton Muslim, *The Moro Armed Struggle in the Philippines* (Marawi City, Philippines: Mindanao State University, 1994), 89-90.

Mindanao continued to have the highest poverty incidence in the country.[16] The "Land of Promise" certainly became a land of fulfillment for Christianized Filipinos and foreign investors, but not for the Moros.[17]

Such dismal conditions imposed upon the Moros by the majority Christian population and the national government inevitably led to violent conflicts in Mindanao. In the early 1970s, the contemporary Moro struggle broke out. By 1976, some 50,000 people had already perished due to the conflict. By the time the Jakarta Peace Agreement between the Philippine government and the Moro National Liberation Front (MNLF) was signed in 1996, more than 150,000 persons had died from the armed clashes, 300,000 buildings and houses had been burned, 535 mosques razed, 35 towns completely wiped out, and half of the entire Moro population uprooted.[18] In the year 2000 alone, when the Philippine government launched an all-out offensive, 439,000 persons were displaced, 6,229 houses razed, and some 2,000 people killed.[19] In August and September 2008, immediately after peace talks broke down between the government and the Moro Islamic Liberation Front (MILF), a battle ensued that claimed more than 100 lives and displaced around 600,000 people.[20]

In terms of population, Muslim Filipinos, who in 1913 formed 98 percent of Mindanao's population, accounted for 40 percent in 1976, and only 19 percent in 1990. In fact, as early as the 1960s, the Moro population had disappeared in many of their long-established areas.[21]

Is it any wonder, then, why the Moros have always felt they are *not* Filipinos?[22] But to Filipino Christians, the Moro historian Alunan

---

[16]Institute of Autonomy and Governance, "ARMM Helps: Synergy in Action," *Autonomy and Peace Review* (April-June 2012): 77-79.

[17]Muslim, *Moro Armed Struggle*, 117-119. A detailed treatment of this subject can be found in Muslim, "The Bangsa Moro: the Highly Neglected People in the Neglected But Rich Mindanao," *Dansalan Quarterly* 12:1-4 (January-December 1992): 59 ff.

[18]Amina Rasul, *Broken Peace?: Assessing the 1996 GRP-MNLF Final Peace Agreement* (Makati City, Philippines, 2007), 5.

[19]Eddie Quitoriano and Theofeliz Marie Francisco, *Their War, Our Struugle: Stories of Children in Mindanao* (Quezon City, Philippines: Save the Children, UK, 2004), 15.

[20]PCID and KAS, *Voices of Dissent: A Postscript to the MOA-AD Decision* (Mandaluyong City, Philippines: PCID and KAS, 2009), iii.

[21]Cesar Adib Majul, *The Contemporary Muslim Movement in the Philippines* (Berkeley, California: Mizan, 1985), 30. See also Policarpo Destura, "A Historical Account of Maranao-Christian Relations, 1935-1972" (M.A. Thesis, University of San Carlos, Cebu City, Philippines, 1981), 70. Destura writes that in Lanao Province the Maranaos who formerly occupied the best lands were displaced methodically and driven farther into the interiors by the new Filipino settlers.

[22]See Abdurassad Asani, *Moros Not Filipinos* (Philippines: Bangsamoro Research Center, n.d.); cited in Muslim, *Moro Struggle,* 132-133. Two surveys were mentioned,

Glang poses these crucial questions: "Where is the moral force of Christianity, the force of love and goodwill to make the Muslim Filipinos feel that they also belong to this nation? Is Christianity good only to convert people and deny . . . the love of Christ? These are questions Christians must answer. These answers will determine whether national cohesiveness is possible."[23]

The Eucharist as Paradigm for Economic Justice

In "unpacking" the idea that the Eucharist is a paradigm for economic justice, let me glean from the insights of John H. Yoder and Monika Hellwig.

In his work *Body Politics*,[24] Yoder underlines the social significance of the Lord's Supper as exemplified in the early Jerusalem church's practice of bread breaking (Acts 2:46). From the meal table, the sharing was extended to a point wherein no one claimed ownership of his possessions (Acts 4:32). To the disciples who participated with Jesus in those meals, it was a typical occurrence: "The sharing was rather the normal, organic extension from table fellowship . . . it was merely the resumption of the way they had been living together with Jesus."[25] The story of the manna in the desert, the reference in Luke 8:3 that speaks of how Jesus' itinerant band was fed through donations, was among the antecedents of the sharing that became normative in the early church's practice of bread breaking.

Yoder's view of the Lord's Supper is basically economic in nature. The early Christians in Jerusalem thus reorganized their leadership pattern to effect a more equitable economic distribution to include non-Palestinian widows (Acts 6). Hence, the Supper is not mere 'symbol-making' wherein from the act a different meaning can be derived; nor is it just sacramental that gives the act a divinely-derived meaning, which accentuates the distance between that special meaning and the ordinary meaning of the act.[26] Rather, Yoder emphasizes the economic aspect of the Supper, stating: "It is that bread *is* daily sustenance.

---

one in 1970 and another in 1984, both of which reported that a majority of the Muslim respondents preferred not to be called Filipinos. The same observation was made by Saleeby in 1903 that the "Moros do not consider themselves Filipinos."

[23]Alunan C. Glang, *Muslim Secession or Integration?* (Quezon City, Philippines: Garcia, 1969), 13; quoted in McAmis, "Muslim Filipinos," 54.

[24]Yoder, *Body Politics: Five Practices of the Christian Community Before the Watching World* (Scottsdale, Arizona: Herald, 1992).

[25]Ibid., 17.

[26]John H. Yoder, "Sacrament as Social Process: Christ the Transformer of Culture," *Theology Today* 48, no. 1 (April 1991): 38.

Bread eaten together *is* economic sharing. Not merely symbolically, but also in fact."[27]

The Lord's Supper is also revolutionary when seen in the light of the Jubilee celebration. Following André Trocmé,[28] Yoder writes that Jesus' platform proclamation in Luke 4, based on Isaiah 61 ("proclaiming the acceptable year of the Lord"), referred to the Mosaic provisions of the Jubilee that involved cancelling debts, redistributing property, and freeing prisoners.[29] This linkage of the Eucharist to the Jubilee is certainly valuable, for "It protects the 'table fellowship' witness from being limited to the level of consumption, without attention to productive resources. The Jubilee is justice on the level of productive capital."[30] Moreover, the redistribution of properties in Leviticus 25 (cf. Deut. 15) points to Jesus' vision that extended beyond kinship groups. It was an inclusive proclamation that the Messiah will bring about not just spiritual, but also the economic well-being of persons "in whatever form that would need to take in the messianic age."[31]

Connecting this economic breaking of bread with the Pauline understanding of the Lord's Supper in 1 Corinthians 11, Yoder maintains: "Eucharist, thus substantially and historically, functionally understood, is the paradigm for every other mode of inviting the outsider and the underdog to the table, whether we call that the epistemological privilege of the oppressed or cooperation or equal opportunity or socialism."[32]

The breaking of the bread is therefore paradigmatic for the preferential option for the poor—i.e., at the Lord's Table, those who have are to bring and share bread so that all can be fed. This kind of sharing is "the model for the Christian social vision in all times and

---

[27]Ibid., 37. Yoder, however, does not deny that the *body practices* were not revealed from above or were created from scratch. "Each was created from already existent cultural models . . . yet in the gospels they have taken on new meanings and a new empowerment" (p. 42). Cf. Yoder's *Body Politics,* 20; *For the Nations: Essays Evangelical and Public* (Grand Rapids, Michigan: Eerdmans, 1997), 44.

[28]André Trocmé, *Jesus and the Nonviolent Revolution* (Scottsdale, Arizona: Herald, 1974). See chapters 2 and 3.

[29]Yoder, *Body Politics,* 24. Cf. Yoder, *The Politics of Jesus: Vicit Agnus Noster* (Grand Rapids, Michigan: Eerdmans, 1972; reprint, Eerdmans, 1980) 34-41.

[30]Yoder, *Body Politics,* 24.

[31]Ibid., 25.

[32]Yoder, *For the Nations,* 32.

places."[33] A similar perspective is held by Monika Hellwig in her work, *The Eucharist and the Hunger of the World*.[34]

There are, says Hellwig, two principal types of hunger: the first concerns *physical sustenance*; the second is hunger for *creative love*. The first type is quite common for us here in the Philippines; everywhere we go, we can see people who are "hungering" for physical sustenance. People who feel this hunger know that it relates to their total experience, which is "brutalizing because it constricts, shortens vision, cuts off the freedom to transcend, which is human."[35] Thus, they understand more deeply the necessity of human interdependence. They "know that their lives are hostages in others' hands—not only their sheer survival but the quality of their lives, the extent of their freedom to be human."[36] However, their drive to be human is often met with frustration, as the persons they need to depend on lack the empathy to help the hungry. The reason for this indifference, Hellwig observes, is not because they lack the material resources to help, but that they themselves are unsatisfied and hungry for authentic, creative love.

Love that is creative is teleological, which means having a person's good in view. Loving creatively, like the Good Samaritan, means helping a person cross over from an existence defined by childish self-centeredness to a life that is empathic and engaged. Consequently, those whose hunger for creative love is left unfulfilled are the ones who amass and waste so much of the world's resources and keep so many others on the edge of starvation. Both are starving, both are not free; but the physically hungry can nevertheless be rescued only if the love-starved persons undergo an experience of genuine conversion from being a person or community of apathy to one of compassion.[37]

Ultimately, for Hellwig and Yoder, the answer to both kinds of hunger is Jesus, whose person, teachings, and actions are embodied in the Church's practice of the Eucharist. Hellwig's view of Jesus as the "Bread of Life" is key to understanding further the economic dimension of the practice. She maintains that, in comparing himself to the manna in the desert (Jn. 6:25 ff.; cf. Exod. 16), Jesus emphasized that what he gives is true sustenance from God, which must be received

---

[33]Ibid., 44.

[34]Monika K. Hellwig, *The Eucharist and the Hunger of the World* (New York: Paulist Press, 1976).

[35]Ibid., 13. See also Monika Hellwig, "The Eucharist and World Hunger," *Word and World* 17, no. 1 (Winter 1997): 65-66. The physically hungry includes people who are grossly underpaid, malnutrition children, the unemployed, and homeless people.

[36]Ibid., 16.

[37]Ibid., 18. Cf. Hellwig, "The Eucharist," 65-66.

as a gift. Like manna, God's gift must not be hoarded or taken coercively to enrich oneself and impoverish others. Thus, Hellwig remarks, "We are God's guests, invited to make the most of the divine hospitality and to mediate it to one another and to the rest of creation."[38] Discipleship is here certainly signified. Yoder says on this point that the "newness of the believing community is the promise of newness on the way for the world."[39] For the believers, Jesus is the "food of life" through whom they discover that hunger for creative love is only satiated by living for others.[40] For this reason, the early Christians broke bread and shared with those in need. Furthermore, Hellwig says:

> When the eucharistic action is seen not only in the context of the farewell supper but in the light of the whole ministry of Jesus, the exigence becomes sharper. Jesus invited his followers into his own redemptive action—a ministry that was constantly among the poor and outcast, concerned with their spiritual and material needs. To accept his eucharistic hospitality entails solidarity with these concerns, respon-ding to the needs of our time and situation. The very existence of hunger and want in our world coupled with our ability to respond would be call enough to practice in the world what we symbolize in the eucharist.[41]

Jesus' ministry and his (the Lord's) Supper certainly do not deal only with the spiritual dimension of the person; they also involve satisfying concretely the hunger of the poor for physical sustenance. A central idea in the Lord's Supper is responsibility for others; the eucharistic sharing of bread and wine, as Yoder correctly points out, "is both specimen and symbol of responsibility."[42] The Church as responsible receiver and bearer of the new life in Christ must have the penetrating insight that humanity's interdependence entails serving and defending the rights of the needy and oppressed.

Finally, from Yoder and Hellwig we learn that the implicit and explicit witness of the Church must be marked by creativity and love, for the Lord's Supper is a paradigm of compassionate sharing. On this point, Yoder remarks that, "Only local discernment can tell which

---

[38]Monika K. Hellwig, *Guests of God: Stewards of Divine Creation* (Mahwah: Paulist Press, 1999), 11.
[39]Yoder, *Body Politics*, 21.
[40]Ibid., 32.
[41]Hellwig, "The Eucharist," 64.
[42]Yoder, *Body Politics*, 22.

angle of attack on economic discrimination is most fitting."[43] Indeed, it is left to the discernment of the Church as it is situated concretely (i.e., in its local context) how it would be able to "touch the lives of the hungry of the world with authentic and generous compassion, drawing on the bread of life that is Jesus, to become themselves bread of life for the needy."[44]

Eucharistic Justice as a Christ-Centered Response to the Bangsamoro Question

The "Moro Problem," as we have seen, is a matter of injustice to the Moro people. In presenting the Eucharist as a response to the Bangsamoro question, I am not, of course, inviting our Muslim neighbors to the ecclesial ritual act of bread breaking. Rather, I seek to invite fellow Christians toward a more agonizing reflection on how participating in the Lord's Supper is a call for us to act justly toward our Muslim neighbors. Hellwig's view on this point is incisive:

> We have sometimes spoken and acted as though the Eucharist had meaning in isolation from the rest of life—as though participation in it guarantees growth in grace independently of the manner in which the participants live their lives in the world. Yet people who participate reverently and frequently in the Eucharist, but drive hard bargains against the weak, taking advantage of the misfortunes of others to enrich themselves . . . are confronted by the prophetic denunciation of both Testaments . . . there is no such thing as growth in grace through participation in the Eucharist where this is isolated from a lifestyle which is a progressive awareness and concern for the suffering of all the oppressed.[45]

As we know, the Moro ancestral land is the crucial element in forging peace in Mindanao. Quite understandably so, for the Philippine government's past policies of what Michael O. Mastura calls "elimination of minority group by emigration," if successful, would lead to none other than the utter dissolution of Moro political and economic power in their native homeland.[46] Without land, debilitating

---

[43]Yoder, *Body Politics*, 25. Cf. Hellwig, *The Eucharist*, 85-87.
[44]Hellwig, *The Eucharist*, 85.
[45]Hellwig, *Eucharist and Hunger*, 58-59.
[46]Michael O. Mastura, "The Mindanao Crisis and Our Congress" (paper presented at the Second National Islamic Symposium, Marawi City, Philippines, 28 April-1 May, 1972), Gowing Memorial Research Center, Marawi City.

hunger will be the Moro's relentless companion. Some forty years ago, the Filipino Christian statesman Raul S. Manglapus implored the government to stop the waves of Christian settlers from acquiring lands in Mindanao. Muslims, he reasoned, have land ownership traditions that must not be trampled upon despite widely-accepted legal practices.[47] But alas, large tracts of lands were already in the hands of many Filipino Christians by that time.

Regarding justice in the sphere of productive capital,[48] the Jubilee's linkage to the Eucharist is relevant. Although originally intended for the Hebrews, it was not irrelevant to those outside of Israel. Indeed, Jesus' meals with society's poor and marginalized make clear that the concern of Jubilee and Eucharistic justice is the restorative distribution of resources for the "economic and personal well-being" of any needy individual or collective person.[49]

In light of the Jubilee, applying eucharistic sharing to the Moro ancestral land issue places present-day Filipinos in a situation that can be likened to the wealthy Jewish lenders during Jesus' time who frequently made use of the *Prosboul* in order to circumvent justice according to the Jubilee.[50] As followers of Jesus, Filipino Christians are confronted with the situation wherein the Jubilee bids us to support the restoration of Moro land to its rightful owners. Should Filipino Christians, then, continue to use the *Prosboul*, which means placing hurdles to the Bangsamoro claim to their lands and to other rights to which they are entitled? Or should we follow the demands of economic justice as announced in the Jubilee proviso of the Eucharist and support the claims of the Muslim people? While negotiations and the subsequent implementation of the peace agreement rest largely upon the leading authorities of the government and the Bangsamoro, I believe the support of Filipino Christians is necessary for its long-term success. It will not certainly suffice for the Church to issue mere

---

[47]Raul S. Manglapus, "Towards a Muslim-Christian Manifesto," in *Christian-Muslim Democracy: Wave of the Future*, ed. Amado Lagdameo (Pasig City, Philippines: Pandan, 1991), 78-79. Manglapus' material was delivered as a speech during a seminar in 1972. See also Hilario Gomez, *The Moro Rebellion and the Search for Peace: A Study on Christian-Muslim Relations in the Philippines* (Zamboanga City, Philippines: Silsilah, 2000), 105-110; 178-181; 185-187.

[48]Yoder, *Body Politics*, 24.

[49]Ibid., 25. See also Karen Lebacqz, "Justice, Economics, and the Uncomfortable Kingdom: Reflections on Matthew 20:1-16," *Annual of the Society of Christian Ethics* (1983): 41; Yoder, *Politics*, 64 ff.

[50]Trocmé, *Jesus and the Nonviolent Revolution*, 42-48.; also in Yoder's *Politics*, 66-74. The *Prosboul* was the legal instrument that the rabbi Hillel crafted that allowed the creditor to collect a debt through the use of the court after the debt was abolished by the Jubilee.

statements such as the preferential option for the poor. What matters is *being* concretely a Church for the Muslim poor.[51]

Economic solidarity for and with our Bangsamoro neighbors will inevitably take on various forms. As Yoder and Hellwig assert, the discernment of the local faith community is necessary because deprivation and hunger, too, have different forms and meanings.[52] The Silsilah Dialogue Movement in Zamboanga, to use it as a fine example, therefore cultivates in various ways a "culture of dialogue" among Muslims and Christians through a process of personal and social transformation.[53] Toward this end Sislilah's various activities, programs, and initiatives are aimed, such as the Harmony Prayer, Peace and Development Services, the Silsilah Forum, and others.[54]

An excellent demonstration of Silsilah's economic solidarity with the Muslims of Mindanao occurred in the September 2013 siege of Zamboanga City, a month which for many was a "September to remember."[55] For twenty days in that fateful month (from the 9th to the 28th), the Misuari Faction of the MNLF laid siege to Zamboanga City. The rebels razed approximately 10,000 houses, displaced thousands of Muslims, and killed hundreds of Muslims and Christians alike.[56] Silsilah responded in various ways. They fed lactating mothers as well as children and other evacuees;[57] they also provided house materials, helped in redeeming lands, surveyed properties at affordable prices, and built transitory tents and houses for those who do not own land.[58] In addition, Silsilah welcomed in its "Harmony Village" some of the sick from Zamboanga City Medical Center, where they received treatment

---

[51] Eliseo R. Mercado, *Southern Philippines Question* (Cotabato City, Philippines: Notre Dame University, 1999),124-125. See also Jubair, *Endless Tyranny*, 265. Jubair invites the many good-hearted Christians to spread the gospel of love by struggling for Moro justice and not let the greedy among them to get the best of Mindanao at the expense of its native inhabitants.

[52] Yoder, *Body Politics*, 25; Hellwig, *Eucharist and Hunger*, 85-87.

[53] See Sebastiano D'Ambra, *A Path to Peace: Culture of Dialogue as Path to Peace* (Zamboanga City, Philippines: Silsilah, 2014), ix ff.

[54] See Sebastiano D'Ambra, *Call to a Dream: Silsilah Dialogue Movement* (Zamboanga City, Philippines: Silsilah, 2008) 68-94.

[55] This phrase is the title of a book that Silsilah published to commemorate the first year anniversary of the Zamboanga Crisis. Available from https://drive.google.com/file/d/0B-1h_u-O7rWwQzd2MG92T3R6Z1k/ view?pli=1 (accessed October 20, 2014). This online version does not contain page numbers.

[56] Silsilah, *September to Remember*. The damages to the directly affected areas, particularly the barangays of Sta. Catalina, Sta. Barbara, Rio Hondo and Mariki, can be likened to those in World War II on a smaller scale. Mariki was left only with the sea. Cecil Bernal, "The Last Cup," in ibid.

[57] Bernal, "Last Cup."

[58] Jirmalyn T. Maad, "Keeping the Faith," in ibid.

by the hospital staff.[59] Indeed, in carrying out such eucharistic initiatives, it is crucial that Christians "enter into their need and find ways to satisfy their hunger"[60] in order to discern the real needs of our hungry and oppressed Bangsamoro neighbors.

Conclusion

"Do this in remembrance of me." Remembering is certainly central to the Lord's Supper practice. It is not, of course, just any kind of remembrance that is important, but one that is linked with responsibility. By *responsible remembrance* I mean to underline our readiness to confront memories of oppressions and be responsible for whatever may have been our part in those "remembered situations."

For us Christian Filipinos, a responsible eucharistic remembrance of Moro-Christian relations means to act based on a truthful interpretation of our own part in the conflict. It means remembering rightly the past and acting justly in the present. "Healing the past" is the foremost challenge, says Antonio Ledesma, which comes not by denying what has happened, but by understanding the root causes of conflict, asserting the equal dignity of every person and community, and redressing injustices whenever possible.[61] For when left unhealed, memories of oppressions will veil persistently the humanity of the other, and so lock both victim and perpetrator into vicious cycles of exclusion and non-reconciliation.[62] Such has mostly been the past narrative of Christians and Muslims in the Philippines. Hence, with the new peace agreement embodied in the Bangsamoro Basic Law that, hopefully, Congress will soon pass into law, we Christians should commit to forging a new narrative with our Moro neighbors that is founded on justice. As Robert Schreiter points out, healing traumatic memories created by conflict cannot be achieved through suppression:

> Rather, over time these memories must come to be embedded in new narratives that do not continue to generate negative emotion. This may be done by establishing a pattern of

---

[59]Aminda E. Saño, "Padayon! (Move On)," in ibid.

[60]Hellwig, *Eucharist and Hunger*, 87.

[61]Antonio Ledesma, *Healing the Past, Building the Future: Soundings From Mindanao* (Quezon City, Philippines: Jesuit Communications, 2005), 42.

[62]Miroslav Volf, *Exclusion and Embrace: A Theological Exploration of Identity, Otherness, and Reconciliation.* Nashville, Tennessee: Abingdon, 1996), 132-133.

meaning in a new narrative whereas in the old one the traumatic event had been the death of meaning.[63]

---

[63]Robert Schreiter, "Sharing Memories of the Past: The Healing of Memories and Interreligious Encounter," *Currents in Theology and Mission* 35, no. 2 (April 2008): 113.

POWER TO THE POOR: TOWARDS A PENTECOSTAL THEOLOGY OF SOCIAL ENGAGEMENT

By Ivan Satyavrata

The extraordinary success of the Pentecostal movement is largely due to its outreach to those on the periphery of society. Some see the reasons for this success as due to sociological factors; others see it in essentially the "power" factor associated with the Holy Spirit's dynamic empowerment. The Pentecostal message is very good news among the poor; it answers their immediate felt needs and provides powerful spiritual impetus and community support for a better life. Several recent studies have shown that the intervention of Pentecostal mission into severely deprived communities unleashes powerful redemptive forces resulting in upward social mobility of believers. The genius of Pentecostalism has thus been its relevance to the powerless—its ability to penetrate the enslaving power structures of the socially and economically marginalized.

Although Pentecostals have from their outset been deeply involved in works of compassion, they have in general been better at doing it than articulating it in statements of faith or theological formulations. Thus Doug Petersen, writing just over a decade ago, laments the fact that despite the substantial contribution of the Assemblies of God to social involvement, "a certain 'gap' exists between pragmatic compassionate outreach and an adequate understanding of biblical foundations which must guide these actions."[1] Petersen's own work in this area has contributed significantly towards bridging this gap.

Dr. George O. Wood, Chairman of the World Assemblies of God Fellowship and General Superintendent of the Assemblies of God, USA, observes, "It's probably been the nature of the Pentecostal experience that we have the experience first and then develop the rationale!"[2] A statement issued at the conclusion of the European

---

[1]Douglas Petersen, "Missions in the Twenty-First Century: Toward a Methodology of Pentecostal Compassion," *Transformation* 16:2 (April 1999]: 54.
[2]George O. Wood, *Letter to Dr. Joseph Dimitrov*, March 29, 2010.

Pentecostal Theological Association on the theme "Pentecostals and Justice" in July 2010, observed the following:

> We agree that our heritage as Pentecostals demonstrates a profound concern for works of mercy, justice and compassion for the poor and that the Full Gospel that we have historically proclaimed addresses the whole range of human need, be it spiritual, physical or social. However, we recognize that we have only of late rediscovered the implications of what that means in terms of our holistic mission to the world.[3]

There were, however, some features of Pentecostal belief and practice which mitigated a proper theology of social engagement, most of which were a carry-over from the fundamentalist antecedents of many early Pentecostals. Some reasons why social action was not prominent on the theological radar of Pentecostals were:[4]

1. Millennial eschatology - Pentecostals came at a time when "evangelicals" didn't have time to think about building the kingdom of God, because of their conviction of the imminent return of Christ and the shift towards a pre-millennial position. Apocalyptic doomsday scenarios with the inevitable impetus towards "otherworldliness" leave little room for concern about social engagement.
2. The rise of old liberalism and the social gospel tended to taint Pentecostal, Holiness, and Evangelical involvement with issues of social justice. As Pentecostals rubbed shoulders with Evangelicals they also adopted the values and concerns of Evangelicals who stood against the liberals who employed the social gospel.
3. Dualism – Again in reaction to reductionist tendencies in modernist versions of Christian mission which highlighted this-worldly, physical benefits of the gospel, Pentecostals sought to give priority to the salvation of the "soul."
4. Apolitical posture – Pentecostals seemed reluctant to integrate anything in their doctrinal statements that seemed politically tainted. Both the Assemblies of God and the Church of God (Cleveland) for instance took a strong pacifistic position during World War I, though not explicitly expressed in their

---

[3]EPTA Statement on Pentecostals and Justice, Mattersey Hall College and Graduate School, England (July 9, 2010].
[4]Cecil M. Robeck, Jr., (Editorial), Pentecostals and Social Ethics, *Pneuma: The Journal of the Society for Pentecostal Studies*, Volume 9:2. (Fall 1987): 106.

statement of faiths developed during those very turbulent years.

Other challenges included the impact of the prosperity gospel which, by postulating almost a *karma* like cause-effect relationship between faith and material wealth, implied that the poor deserve their status. Furthermore, concern for practical social needs was commonly viewed by Pentecostals as a natural inseparable part of evangelism, and hence they never felt the need to develop a distinct theology for it. A final observation worth noting in this regard is that as a revival movement, Pentecostalism was in general less concerned about developing theology than it was about seeing the Holy Spirit infuse the Church with spiritual vibrancy and a burden for world evangelization. The limited theological concerns of Pentecostals were thus devoted to providing biblical justification of their distinctive doctrinal emphasis on the baptism in the Holy Spirit and related teachings. While there is no denying the fact that, especially in the early stages of the movement, the urgency to evangelize tended to blur the vision for social justice, right from the beginning Pentecostals have also excelled in various kinds of social programs.[5]

Whatever the reasons for the lack of adequate articulation of a theology of social concern, it is impossible to deny that social engagement is today an essential component of the Pentecostal missionary movement in most regions of the world. As an astute researcher observes, "...engagement in social ministry by Pentecostals has practically exploded in the last few decades."[6] But is this a welcome development? Is this the result of the Holy Spirit's leading or something that Pentecostals have wandered into inadvertently? How firmly is this trend anchored in Scripture? When Pentecostals embrace this heightened emphasis on social engagement, are they being faithful to the roots of their tradition or are they merely yielding to cultural pressures?

Whether or not we agree with those who would view this as an unhealthy trend, the questions raised are not only valid, but vital for the future of the movement, and highlight the need for us to develop a cogent and cohesive Pentecostal theology of social engagement. A task of this nature is necessarily both communal and cumulative: *communal* because it has to emerge from an ongoing conversation within the global Pentecostal community; and consequently *cumulative*, because it

---

[5]Velli Matti, "Spirituality and Social Justice."
[6]Kent Duncan, "Emerging Engagement: The Growing Social Conscience of Pentecostalism," *Encounter: Journal for Pentecostal Ministry* 7 (Summer 2010): 2.

must bring together perspectives that reflect the various contextual Spirit-illuminated readings of Scripture and the actual experience and praxis of Pentecostal reflective practitioners in different regions of the world. What follows must be viewed as a modest contribution to this ongoing conversation.

Our strategy in outlining a theology of social engagement both builds on the two earlier presentations and carries it forward. To begin with, we must ensure that our theology emerges from, and is in close alignment with, the clear teaching of Scripture. "If this engagement of social responsibility exists as a legitimate expression of Pentecostal ministry, then it must reflect biblical roots and align with sound biblical doctrine."[7] Our consideration of the biblical material which shapes our understanding of Pentecostal mission in the previous lecture has helped us lay a foundation for this.

Secondly, although Scripture is our final authority in any theological formulation, it helps our case if we can draw corroborative support from the testimony of history. A robust theological formulation will explore the sources of Christian tradition and glean what it can from the insights of the fathers of the faith. The witness of those who lived closest to the apostolic era is especially helpful in this regard.

Thirdly, we focus on the distinctive theological resources of the Pentecostal movement itself, in particular, Pentecostal spirituality. Pentecostal theological thinking and action springs from a transforming spiritual experience (a distinctive second work of the Spirit), usually evidenced by speaking in tongues, given for an endowment of spiritual "power" for witness and/or to be active participants in God's mighty works. This experience provides a sense of the nearness and redemptive power of God's Spirit break into our life today. We evaluate briefly how this Pentecostal experience helps shape the Pentecostal social conscience and social engagement.

A Biblically Rooted Social Ethic

The Genesis account of creation is designed to show among other things that humankind was the climax of God's creation program. In the first recorded encounter between God and Adam and Eve in Genesis 1:28, God blesses their existence and defines their role in creation. The following two verses describe God's provision for them and all living creatures. This means that God's first word to human beings is a word of direction; the second word is a word of provision, indicating God's intention that all of humankind are provided for in

---

[7]Duncan, "Emerging Engagement," 4.

their journey of life. Poverty is thus a contradiction of God's primary intention that the basic living needs of all of humanity are properly provided for. Both Old and New Testaments clearly support this assertion that God in his providence seeks the subsistence and survival of all his creatures (Ps 104; Ex 16; Matt 6:32-33; Acts 14:17). Hence, poverty is not in itself a blessing; it contradicts God's primary intention of providence.

Murray Dempster summarizes the Old Testament (OT) basis for a Christian social ethics in three convincing arguments.[8] In the first place he argues that Christian theological reflection must be grounded in God's self-revelation of himself and his character. God reveals himself repeatedly and unmistakably in the OT as a God who is especially concerned with the needs of the poor and the powerless, and may even be viewed as possessing a "preferential" bias for the poor against the rich. Secondly, the biblical concept of the *Imago Dei* obliges us to value all human beings as created in the image of God. Our social ethic should thus flow out of our desire to treat with respect and dignity all other human beings who are also made in the image of God.

Thirdly, the unilateral Sinai covenant between God and Israel indicates that God is not merely concerned about our salvation, but also with the well-being of his creation. The Ten Commandments show that a right relation with God (Ex 20:3-11) should be complemented by a right relationship with people in society (Ex 20:12-17). The law and the covenant were a prescription of what life should look like for the people of God. The ministry of the prophets reminded God's people of what it means to live according to his character. Israel's socio-ethical actions were to thus demonstrate God's nature and character. God's covenant people were chosen to reflect who God is and what he does.

The nation of Israel was thus explicitly commanded by God to imitate God's special concern for the poor and oppressed (Ex 22:21-24; Deut 10:17-18; 15:13-15). This command is echoed in the New Testament (NT) in Jesus' teaching to his followers to imitate God's mercy and kindness (Luke 6:33-36), as well as in apostolic instructions to the Church to give generously to the needy (1 John 3:16-18), as evidence of authentic Christian discipleship (James 1:27). Not only that, the Bible also expressly warns God's people against neglect or mistreatment of the poor and the oppressed, in OT prophetic

---

[8] Murray W. Dempster, "Pentecostal Social Concern and the Biblical Mandate of Social Justice," *Pneuma: The Journal of the Society for Pentecostal Studies*, Volume 9:2. (Fall 1987): 130-137.

admonitions (Isa 1:10-17; 58:3-7; Amos 5:21-24) as well as NT exhortations (Luke 1:46-53; 4:18; 6:20-25; Mark 12:38-40; James 5:1-6).

Jesus and the poor were, of course, inseparable. The needy flocked around him everywhere he went: the beggars, the sick, the destitute, the bereaved, the hungry masses, and he was always touched by their needs. Ten times the NT records that Jesus was "moved with compassion," and each time it was when he was confronted with suffering people. We have already looked briefly at Jesus' teaching concerning the kingdom of God, which is the unifying theme that provides a description of what life would look like under God's redemptive kingdom reign. Firmly within the tradition of the prophets, Jesus teaches and embodies through his parables and miracles, what life in the kingdom should look like—a life marked by justice, mercy, love, and peace.

The kingdom, the central theological concept used by Luke in his gospel to describe Jesus' mission and ministry, is the connective between the Luke-Acts account. "Those things which Jesus began to do and teach . . ." (Acts 1:1) both summarizes his earthly ministry and sets the agenda for the ministry of the apostles subsequent to their receiving the transfer of the Spirit. In effect the kingdom mission of Jesus (including his kingdom ethic) is transferred to the charismatic community by the descent of the Spirit at Pentecost. The kingdom ethic of Jesus is made operational within the charismatic community by the empowerment of the Holy Spirit and becomes thereafter the moral foundation for the life of the early church.

The Holy Spirit is presented in the Acts as one who empowers the Church to overcome the entrenched gender, economic, cultural, and religious barriers of a divided world. The book of Acts mentions two immediate results of the outpouring of the Holy Spirit on the Day of Pentecost. First, "many wonders and miraculous signs were done by the apostles" (2:43); and second, "All the believers were together and had everything in common. Selling their possessions and goods, they gave to anyone as he had need" (2:44-45). This is further elaborated in Acts 4:32-35:

> *All the believers were one in heart and mind. No one claimed that any of his possessions was his own, but they shared everything they had. With great power the apostles continued to testify to the resurrection of the Lord Jesus, and much grace was upon them all. There were no needy persons among them. For from time to time those who owned lands or houses sold them, brought the money from the sales and put it at the apostles' feet, and it was distributed to anyone as he had need.*

In Acts 2, the *gender* distinctions of male and female were overcome by the empowerment of the Spirit. Also in Acts 2 but detailed further in Acts 4 and 5, the *economic* distinctions between rich and poor were overcome in the economic *koinonia* established by the power of the Spirit. In Acts 10, the *cultural* distinctions between Jew and Gentile were overcome within the Christian community by the coming of the Spirit. Acts 9:36 refers to the disciple Tabitha from Joppa "...who was always doing good and helping the poor." When the prophet Agabus predicted a devastating famine, "The disciples, each according to his ability, decided to provide help for the brothers living in Judea" (Acts 11:29). The Book of Acts demonstrates that the preaching of the gospel resulted in a loving community, where they felt responsible to meet both spiritual and material needs.

This finds resonance in the rest of the New Testament. In his letter to the Galatians, Paul mentions that the one thing which the apostles asked him and Barnabas to do as they ministered to the gentiles was that "...we should continue to remember the poor" (Gal. 2:10). In his closing remarks he admonishes the Galatians, "Let us do good to all people, especially to those who belong to the family of believers" (Gal. 6:10). Paul's instructions to Titus also have "good works" as a central theme and concludes with the exhortation, "Our people must learn to devote themselves to doing what is good, in order to provide for urgent needs and not live unproductive lives" (Titus 3:14; cf. 2:7; 3:8). James is very explicit in his appeal to demonstrate our faith by good works, when he states, "faith by itself, if it is not accompanied by action, is dead" (James 2:17), and "to look after orphans and widows in their distress" as a mark of a "pure and faultless religion" (James 1:27). In his letters, John interprets compassion as the practical translation of God's love, "If anyone has material possessions and sees his brother in need but has no pity on him, how can the love of God be in him? Dear children, let us not love with words or tongue but with actions and in truth" (1 John 3:17-18).

The full significance of the NT Church's appropriation of the kingdom ethic of Jesus must not be diluted. Its purpose was to confirm the validity of the claim that the gospel had the power to institute in the practice of the believing community the kingdom ethic of Jesus, which fulfilled the Old Testament proclamation for social justice to reign. This establishment of a just community governed by the Holy Spirit is used apologetically by Luke to demonstrate that the Church was established by the exalted Jesus Christ (Acts 2:33, 4:32-37, 10:24-48). The Church's social ethic and engagement is thus not merely a helpful appendage to the Church's witness, but an essential and integral part of it. The Church's social witness, in fact, authenticates its verbal witness—works and wonders must always complement word.

A Historically Attested Social Conscience

A detailed treatment is beyond the scope of this paper, but the following illustrations should suffice as evidence that the Church's social conscience remained active through the early years of its history. Justin Martyr wrote in 151 AD:

> And they who are well to do, and willing, give what each thinks fit; and what is collected is deposited with the president, who succors the orphans and widows and those who, through sickness or any other cause, are in want, and those who are in bonds and the strangers sojourning among us, and in a word takes care of all who are in need.[9]

A few decades later in 195 AD Tertullian observes in his *Apologeticus*:

> Though we have our treasure-chest, it is not made up of purchase-money, as of a religion that has its price. On the monthly day, if he likes, each puts in a small donation; but only if it be his pleasure, and only if he be able: for there is no compulsion; all is voluntary. These gifts are, as it were, piety's deposit fund. For they are not taken thence and spent on feasts, and drinking-bouts, and eating-houses, but to support and bury poor people, to supply the wants of boys and girls destitute of means and parents, and of old persons confined now to the house; such, too, as have suffered shipwreck; and if there happen to be any in the mines, or banished to the islands, or shut up in the prisons, for nothing but their fidelity to the cause of God's Church, they become the nurslings of their confession.[10]

In his classic treatment of *The Mission and Expansion of Christianity in the First Three Centuries,* researched over a century ago, Adolf Harnack meticulously documented the works of charity of

---

[9]Justin Martyr, The Fist Apology – Chapter 67: http://www.ccel.org/ccel/schaff/anf01.viii.ii.lxvii.html (Accessed September 26, 2015).

[10]Tertutllian, *Apology,* Chapter 39: http://www.newadvent.org/fathers/0301.htm (Accessed September 26, 2015).

the early church. Harnack was convinced that the early church's social witness was a critical factor which contributed to its extraordinary growth. Harnack categorizes his profuse references from early church sources into ten areas of social involvement:

1. Alms in general, and their connection with the cultus and officials of the church.
2. The support of teachers and officials.
3. The support of widows and orphans.
4. The support of the sick, the infirm, and the disabled.
5. The care of prisoners and people languishing in the mines.
6. The care of poor people needing burial, and of the dead in general.
7. The care of slaves.
8. The care of those visited by great calamities.
9. The churches furnishing work, and insisting upon work.
10. The care of brethren on a journey (hospitality), and of churches in poverty or any peril.[11]

Harnack's work is a gold-mine of research both for its wealth of detail and the breadth of insights it offers into the social witness of the early church. For our purpose it offers indisputable evidence that an active social conscience and earnest social engagement was a vital feature of the Church's life through the earliest years of its existence.

A Socially Transforming Spirituality[12]

The main distinguishing mark of Pentecostalism is its spirituality. The theme of the Holy Spirit's empowerment has always been at the heart of Pentecostal belief: "But you will receive power when the Holy Spirit comes on you; and you will be my witnesses . . . " (Acts1:8).

---

[11] Adolf Harnack, The *Mission and Expansion of Christianity in the First Three Centuries*, 1908, trans. by James Moffatt, 154-190: http://www.preteristarchive,cin. Books/1908_harnack_expansion. html (Accessed September 26, 2015).

[12] Murray A. Dempster, Byron D. Klaus, and Douglas Petersen, eds., *Called and Empowered: Global Mission of Pentecostal Perspective* (Peabody: Hendrickson Publishers, 1991); Eldin Villafañe, "The Politics of the Spirit: Reflections on a Theology of Social Transformation for the Twenty-First Century," 1996 Presidential Address, *Pneuma: The Journal of the Society for Pentecostal Studies*, vol. 18 (Fall 1996): 161-170; Cecil M. Robeck Jr., "Pentecostals and Social Ethics," *Pneuma*, vol. 9 (Fall 1987): 103-107; Richard J. Mouw, "Life in the Spirit in an Unjust World," *Pneuma*, vol. 9 (Fall 1987):109-128; and Murray W. Dempster, "Pentecostal Social Concern and the Biblical Mandate of Social Justice," *Pneuma,* vol. 9 (Fall 1987): 129-153.

Spirituality—living the life of the Holy Spirit—energizes and enables the Church to witness to the kingdom through evangelization and social engagement. The believer's encounter with the Holy Spirit results in a spiritual transformation that reshapes her moral and social consciousness, causing her to become an instrument of social change. Transformed people are empowered by the Spirit to transform the world in the light of the in-breaking kingdom of God. We will examine how Pentecostal spirituality shapes Pentecostalism's social response as we look at five key features of Pentecostal spirituality.

Prayer/Worship

Individual and corporate prayer and worship experience is a very important feature of Pentecostal spirituality. We have already observed (in our previous lecture) the critical role of prayer in missionary engagement of the powers of evil that hinder the advance of the kingdom. Prayer is in actuality the "cry" of the kingdom in response to Jesus' exhortation to his disciples to pray for the coming of the kingdom (Matt 6:10).

God's kingdom by its very nature is God's gift and work. Believers do not construct the kingdom, but rather ask for it and welcome it. It comes by grace and grows within us by the power of the Spirit. Prayer empowers us and compels us to strive for just and loving relationships among people, in family, in community, and in society. The corporate worship experience of Pentecostals is a crucial element in the shaping of Pentecostal spirituality and is a crucial stage in social engagement when directed towards kingdom advancement and in opposition to the powers of evil.

Liberation

The Pentecostal experience of Spirit baptism is basically one of empowerment, and the overwhelming reality that this experience opens to believers is liberation from captivity to the powers of evil that keep them from fullness of life. Pentecostals have always understood the empowering of the Holy Spirit as the power "to be" and the power "to do." It is liberating to those existing in the shadows, marginalized from the economic and social center of society, to those whose experience of poverty leaves them feeling helpless and disempowered. Frighteningly powerful and destructive forces that hold the poor captive must yield to the power of the Holy Spirit.

The liberating experience of the power of the Holy Spirit counters the negative experience of power as an inescapable descending spiral.

The gifts of the Spirit empower their recipients "to do" and "to be," negating the significance of popular prerequisites to power, education, wealth and other status symbols. Pentecostals place high value on giftedness and spiritual power. Those who are of no consequence outside of the Church find themselves part of a rapidly growing alternative society in which they are highly esteemed and appreciated because of their giftedness. This experience of liberating empowerment has become the basis for the upward mobility of Pentecostals in society.

Healing

The belief and practice of divine healing has been a vital component of Pentecostal spirituality since the movement's inception and the earliest indisputable pointer to its holistic concern. This is one area in which Pentecostals departed early from the theology of their evangelical and fundamentalist predecessors when they sought to apply the benefits of the atonement of Christ to the whole person—body, soul and spirit. This is one reason why Pentecostals have tended to naturally and easily been moved to respond to the felt physical needs of the poor. It was impossible to believe that God's "real presence" manifested through the power of the Spirit could miraculously heal sick bodies and not want his people to care and respond to the felt physical and social needs of the poor and dispossessed.

Community

One of the signs of the Holy Spirit's empowering presence is *Koinonia*. The word *Koinonia* occurs 18 times in the NT and denotes *that fellowship among believers which the Holy Spirit creates* (2 Cor 13:14; Phil 2:1). The *Koinonia* of the Holy Spirit involved a sharing of a common life within the Church (Acts 2:42-46; 5:42) and is illustrated in its description as the Body of Christ (1 Cor 12). This means that the members of the Body have an obligation within the Body to "*one another*," and these obligations constitute hall-marks of *Koinonia*, marks or signs of the distinctive kingdom lifestyle, such as love, unity, justice, healing, godliness and other gifts and fruit of the Spirit.

The *Koinonia* of the Spirit enables the Church to demonstrate what the reign of God is like, to incarnate the values of the kingdom that Jesus taught. Thus "witnessing" was not something the Church did; it was a function that flowed out of the common life and experience of the Church-as-community. The early church communities did not act from a concept of social justice. The concern they showed for the poor, widows and strangers, was not a separate activity, but rather an extension of their worship and witness.

Spirit-inspired *Koinonia* at the local level has been a powerful agent of social transformation since the beginning of the Pentecostal movement. The strong sense of community, patterned after the model of the early church helps Pentecostals find a new sense of dignity and purpose in life. The *Koinonia* experience of the early Pentecostals resulted in the emergence of communities which functioned as social alternatives that protested against oppressive structures. Their solidarity created affective ties, giving them a sense of equality, and causing them to challenge inequality in the treatment of minorities, women, and the poor. During a time when racial and gender inequality was endemic, Pentecostals welcomed black and white, male and female, rich and poor.

Hope

Pentecostals view their experience of the Spirit in eschatological terms, offering a present foretaste of a promised future (Eph 1:14). Pentecostals believe that they have been called by God in the "last days" (Acts 2:17) to be Christ-like witnesses in the power of the Spirit. The hope in the imminent coming of the Lord has sustained Pentecostals during persecution, harassment, imprisonment and martyrdom during the last century. They have consistently taught that the Church must be ready for the coming of the Lord by means of faithful witness and holy living. Pentecostals today continue to believe that intense hope has been and will continue to be necessary for endurance, healing and engagement of the forces—both social and spiritual—which oppress and violate people.

A common popular understanding of future events presumes the annihilation of the world, and clearly undermines the need for sustained social engagement. But as Kärkkäinen points out, for many Pentecostals eschatological hope has brought with it optimism about the work they are doing to bring about social transformation. They view their efforts as visible "signposts," evidence that the kingdom of God has pressed into the present.[13] Miroslav Volf adds further theological validity to this position on the basis of Rom 8:21 that the liberation of creation cannot occur through its destruction but only through its transformation. He argues that kingdom oriented social projects have eschatological significance, and eschatological continuity

---

[13] Petersen, Pentecostal Compassion, 57.

between God's present reign and the reign to come "guarantees that noble human efforts will not be wasted."

When such eschatological continuity is postulated Pentecostal social engagement takes on different significance with fresh potential for sustaining an enduring vision of eternity as articulated in the words of a leading Pentecostal social ethicist, "Expressions of Christian social concern that are kingdom-signifying deeds of anticipatory transformation are the kinds of human effort that God preserves, sanctifies and directs teleologically toward the future age of God's redemptive reign."[14]

---

[14]Murray W. Dempster, "Christian Social Concern in Pentecostal Perspective" (Presidential address, conference of the Society for Pentecostal Studies, Lakeland, Florida, November 7–9, 1991), 36.

Is She a Sinful Woman or a Forgiven Woman?
An Exegesis of Luke 7:36-50
Part I

By Yuri Phanon

Introduction

The Gospel of Luke is a beautiful book. It contains unique stories that cannot be found in the other Gospels, stories that have fascinated me. At the time I was in Bible School, even though I had never studied theology, Greek, or any issues among the Synoptics, I was able to see that Luke had a special ability to write stories. By reading his product, my faith has grown. After I entered Bible school and seminary, I was engaged in studying historical backgrounds, the Synoptic issues, etc. It made a deep impact on me when I came to know that the Gospels are not merely storybooks that have been preserved from the ancient times but are collections of *pericopes,* and there are intentions and purposes for which the author of each Gospel placed each *pericope* in a particular place in their Gospels. There are four Gospels and each of them reflects the author's understanding of Jesus, the author's purpose, and the readers' needs. At the same time, we are able to see whom Jesus really was to the people who lived in the Jewish culture in the first century, to the readers each Gospel author wrote to and to us who live in this present age. The more we study the Bible, the more we can love Jesus. The more we understand what is behind each story in the Gospels, the more we understand the meaning of the good news. This paper will present who Jesus was to the people of his time, to the readers of the author and to us today. In Luke, we can see a very interesting and significant story (Luke 7:36-50).

There is an issue in this passage. There was a certain woman who wept and wet Jesus' feet with her tears. She kissed them and anointed them. Some pastors and Christians have recognized that since she showed her great love to Jesus; her sins were forgiven. Sometimes, I heard this misinterpretation in Sunday school and church. It caused me great confusion that in order to receive salvation and forgiveness, I should show love or good deeds. Some Bible translations, including

Japanese and English versions, are not correct so I believe that the same confusion has existed among both new believers and mature Christians. I do not support the view that in order to receive forgiveness, I have to love first because as a human, how could we love someone from whom we cannot receive any benefits? It is natural to think that she received something from Jesus before she entered the Pharisee's house. I love Jesus because He came to me first not because I came to Him first and asked Him for forgiveness. I would like to prove and to know when this woman was forgiven by doing an exegesis on this passage. This exegesis will lead us to understand the relationship among love, forgiveness, and salvation in the present time and will reflect the heart of the Gospel, the reason that Jesus came to earth. In this paper, I will present textual criticism, exegesis and applications that can be applied to ones' personal interactions with God and people.

Part I of this paper will discuss the preparation of the Lukan passage, including its relationship to the same passages in the other Synoptic Gospels, a translation of the passage and a textual criticism. Part I will also present my exegesis of the passage from Luke 7:36-43. Part II will present the remainder of my exegesis from 7:44-50, conclusions and applications.

Preparation of Luke 7:36-50

Translation of Luke 7:36-50

Verse 36: And one of the Pharisees requested Jesus in order that he might have dinner with Him. Jesus came into the house of the Pharisee and He reclined at the table.

Verse 37: Then behold! There was a woman who used to be a sinner in the city. And when she knew that Jesus was eating at the house of the Pharisee, she brought an alabaster jar of perfume.

Verse 38: And she set herself behind him at his feet crying she began to wet his feet with the tears, she kept on wiping his feet with the hair of her head, she kept on kissing affectionately to his feet, and kept on anointing them with the perfume.

Verse 39: Now, seeing what the woman was doing to Jesus, the Pharisee who invited Jesus was saying to himself, "If this man were a prophet, He would know who is touching and what kind of woman this is for she is a sinner."

Verse 40: But Jesus answered and said to him, "Simon, I have something to tell you." He said "Teacher, please tell me."

Verse 41: A certain moneylender had two debtors. The one owed five hundred denarii and the other fifty denarii.

Verse 42: They were not able to pay back so the moneylender graciously forgave both. Then which one of them will love the moneylender more?

Verse 43: Simon answered and he said, "I suppose to the one whom he forgave more." And Jesus said to him, "You judged rightly."

Verse 44: And turning to the woman, Jesus said to Simon, "Do you see this woman? When I came to your house, you did not give me water for my feet but she wet my feet with the tears and wiped with her hair.

Verse 45: You did not give me a kiss but she did not cease kissing my feet since the time I came.

Verse 46: You did not anoint my head with olive oil but she anointed my feet with the perfume.

Verse 47: Therefore, I tell you that her many sins have been forgiven, as is evidenced by the fact that she loved much, but the one who is forgiven little loves little."

Verse 48: And Jesus said to the woman, "Your sins have been forgiven."

Verse 49: The ones reclining at the table began to say to themselves, "Who is this man even he forgives sins?"

Verse 50: But Jesus said to the woman, "Your faith has saved you, go in peace."

The Synoptic Gospels

The parallel story with Luke 7:36-50 is seen in the books of Matthew, Mark and John (Matthew 26:6-13, Mark 14:3-9, John 12:1-8). Matthew, Mark, and John told the same story from different perspectives, but I will contend that Luke told a story which is different from the other Gospels so Luke's story is unique. Many scholars, such as Bock[1] and Green,[2] also agree with this assessment although others, such as Marshall[3] and Fitzmyer,[4] say that the story in all four Gospels is the same.

In my view, there are a number of differences that make Luke's story unique. For example, Matthew, Mark and John say this story happened in Bethany but Luke says the story happened in the house of Simon the Pharisee, which was either in Nain or some unknown city.

---

[1] Darrell Bock, *Luke: 1:1-9:50*, (Ada, MI: Baker Books, 1994), 691.

[2] Joel B. Green, *The Gospel of Luke*, (Grand Rapids, MI: Wm. B. Eerdmans, 1997), 305.

[3] I. Howard Marshall, *The Gospel of Luke: A Commentary on the Greek Text* (Kingstown, Broadway: Paternoster Press, 1978), 305–307.

[4] Joseph Fitzmyer, *The Gospel According to Luke I-IX* (Broadway, NY: Doubleday Religious Publishing Group, 1995), 685.

Another example is that both Matthew and Mark do not say anything about the woman's hair. John mentions that she anointed Jesus' feet and used her hair to wipe it. Luke, however, has more details. Luke says that the woman stood behind Jesus weeping and began to wet his feet with her tears, wipe them with her hair, kissed them and poured perfume on them.

Textual Criticism

This textual criticism is based on UBS 4th edition. There are two issues regarding textual criticism in verses 39 and 45. In verse 39, when the woman approached Jesus and anointed him, the Pharisee, Simon, had an assurance that Jesus was not "a" prophet because Jesus allowed the woman to touch Him. The text reads ppοφήτης (meaning "a prophet") but the variant reads ὁ ppοφήτης (meaning "The prophet"). As for the external evidence, many major manuscripts such as A B² D L W D Q f in addition to the church fathers from the 2nd, 4th, 5th, 6th-10th and 11th-16th centuries (e.g. Amphilochius and Chrysostom), follow the text, rather than the variant. On the other hand, only a few manuscripts support the variant reading such as B* X 205. No church fathers support this reading. So in terms of the external evidence, it is quite clear that the reading of the text should be maintained. As for the internal evidence, we need to know the reason why some scribes added "ὁ" to the word ppοφήτης. Some scribes wanted to emphasize that Jesus is the prophet whom the prophets in the Old Testament promised to their people. They wanted to insist that Jesus is not merely "A" prophet but "the" prophet who was sent by God to redeem His people. Deut 18:15. John 1:21, 6:14, and 7:40 also has this reflection.[5] In conclusion, as both the external and internal evidence show, the reading of the text should be maintained.

As for verse 45, the story line is like this: After Jesus told Simon the parable of the two debtors, Jesus began to tell him what he did not do and what the woman did for Jesus. Verse 45 is part of Jesus' teaching. Jesus said to Simon "you did not give me a kiss but this woman, from the time I entered, has not stopped kissing my feet." (NIV) The word "enter" causes some textual problems. The text reads εἰσῆλθον which means, "I (Jesus) entered." On the other hand, the variant reads εἰσῆλθεν, which means "she (the sinful woman) entered." So how will these two different readings affect the exegesis? Actually, it does not really cause a huge difference, but Omanson suggests that the reason why some scribes

---

[5]Roger L. Omanson, *A Textual Guide to the Greek New Testament: An Adaptation of Bruce M. Metzger's Textual Commentary for the Needs of Translators* (Stuttgart: Deutsche Bibelgesellschaf, 2007), 122.

changed the word is that they wanted to avoid an exaggeration. I will explain this after presenting the external evidence.

Regarding the external evidence, a huge number of the manuscripts support the text reading, including A B D L^c W D Q X f f^1 28 33 180 205, etc. Some church fathers such as Chrysostom and Ambrose also support this reading. As for the variant, comparing it to the text, a few minor manuscripts support this reading (L* f ^{13} 157 1071 1243 vg syr $^{p, h, pal}$). Even though Amphilochius and Augustine follow the variant reading, when we look at how the readings are so widely accepted, the variant reading is not acceptable. Obviously, the text reading is more widely accepted and also since the earliest reading is from the second century, it is natural to support the text reading.

Going back to the internal evidence, the reason that some scribes chose to use "she entered" is that they wanted to avoid a misreading and an exaggeration of the text. Some people might misunderstand that when Jesus came in, the woman was already there, at Simon's house, waiting for Jesus and started kissing Him. However, as Luke already explained earlier, it is clear that the woman came after Jesus entered the house.[6]

Exegesis of Luke 7:36-43

Verse 36: Setting

This verse starts with the word Ἠρώτα. The reason that this word is an imperfect form is that this word is naturally used here as background information that sets the scene for the narrative that follows. Here Luke does not use the word "inviting" but "Requesting." The Pharisee initiated to invite Jesus.[7] Jesus was not only a friend of sinners but also of anyone who welcomed Him; He would be there. The Pharisee spontaneously invited Jesus. On the other hand, we can see an uninvited guest, the woman coming into the Pharisee's house in verse 37, τις αὐτὸν τῶν Φαρισαίων. According to Marshall, this Greek word order is unusual suggesting that Luke probably wanted to inform his readers that something unusual would happen at this banquet where Jesus was invited by one of the Pharisees.[8] The reason that the Pharisee invited Jesus for dinner is that Jesus was considered to be a great teacher. However the Pharisee thought more than that. He was greatly interested in Jesus and thought that Jesus might have been a prophet.[9] The way the

---

[6]Ibid.

[7]Martin M. Culy, Mikeal Carl Parsons, and Joshua J. Stigall, *Luke: A Handbook on the Greek Text* (Waco, TX: Baylor University Press, 2010), 240.

[8]Marshall, *The Gospel of Luke*, 307.

[9]David Gooding, *According to Luke: A New Exposition of the Third Gospel* (Downers

Pharisee welcomed Jesus was not warm at all because the Pharisee did not give Jesus water, oil, and a kiss but at least the Pharisee knew that Jesus was trustworthy enough in terms of purity.

To sum up, the Pharisee invited Jesus as an honorable and a great teacher and because he was curious if Jesus was really a prophet. His welcoming was sufficient enough since he had a great meal to offer but we cannot say that he welcomed Jesus to his heart with love since he did not show any extra hospitality to him. It is clear that Luke wanted to show the difference between how the Pharisee and how the woman received Jesus' message and invited Jesus. The Pharisee and the teachers of the law rejected both John the Baptist and Jesus because they strongly believed that if they observed temple practice such as sacrifice, their sins would be forgiven. For them, John the Baptist and Jesus could be interesting teachers but not more than that. The Pharisees and the self-righteous people did feel that they did not need the messages of John the Baptist and Jesus.[10] Journalist Philip Yancey explains this well in his book, *The Jesus I Never Knew* saying, "Perhaps prostitutes, tax collectors, and other known sinners responded to Jesus so readily because at some level they knew they were wrong and to them God's forgiveness looked very appealing."[11] Also C.S. Lewis says in his book *A Mind Awake: An Anthology of C.S. Lewis,* "Prostitutes are in no danger of finding their present life so satisfactory that they cannot turn to God: the proud, the avaricious, the self-righteous, are in that danger."[12]

Verse 37-38: Anointing of Jesus' Feet by the Sinful Woman

In verse 37, Luke tells us that there was a woman who lived a sinful life in the city, and she came to the Pharisee's house. How could it be possible that a sinner entered the Pharisee's "holy" house? At that time, it was common for religious people to open their doors to the poor so the door was not locked or closed when people were having meals. The woman had no hindrance in entering the Pharisee's house. However once the poor were able to manage to enter houses of religious people, they should remain silent and not get close to the place where people had their dinner.[13]

Grove, IL: Inter-Varsity Press, 1987), 138.

[10]Van Til, K. A. 2006. "Three Anointings and One Offering: The Sinful Woman in Luke 7.36-50." *Journal Of Pentecostal Theology* 15, no. 1: 73-82. New Testament Abstracts, EBSCOhost (accessed August 7, 2013)

[11]Philip Yancey, *The Jesus I Never Knew* (Grand Rapids, MI: Zondervan, 1996), 152.

[12]C. S. Lewis, *A Mind Awake: An Anthology of C. S. Lewis* (Boston, MA: Houghton Mifflin Harcourt, 2003), 112.

[13]Craig S. Keener, *The IVP Bible Background Commentary: New Testament* (Downers Grove, IL: InterVarsity Press, 1993), 208–209.

The word ἰδοὺ indicates that the woman's unusual character as a sinner also has a function to get the reader's attention on her.¹⁴ So what kind of unusual character did she have? What kind of job was she involved in? Among scholars there is a debate whether she was a prostitute or not. At that time, people who were considered to be "Sinners" were either to be involved in sinful occupations such as tax collectors, tanners, camel drivers, customs collectors, or in immorality. I agree with the Stein's view that the woman could be a prostitute because of Jesus' announcement of forgiveness over her in 7:47-50. It shows that her sins were not ceremonial matters but immoral ones.¹⁵ However there is no strong evidence that she was a prostitute since Luke did not mention anything about her occupation. I believe that she was a prostitute because of Matthew 21:31. Jesus says, "I tell you the truth, the tax collectors and the prostitutes are entering the kingdom of God ahead of you." However it does not really matter whether or not she was a prostitute. The point here is that she was a sinner. One of the significant themes in the Gospel of Luke is God's salvation. It is one of the reasons why Luke uses the word αμαρτiva a lot compared to Mark and Matthew (e.g. Luke 5:8, 30, 32, 6:32-34, 7:34, 37, 39). Both Mark and Matthew use this word only eleven times¹⁶ while Luke uses it eighteen times. The woman here is described as one of the sinners who accepted Jesus' salvation and forgiveness. This story is one of the significant events showing how salvation came to sinners. Luke wanted to show the difference between how the Pharisee and how the woman received Jesus' message. As I have already mentioned, some interpret this story to mean that her sins were forgiven because she showed great love, but I do not agree with this view. This woman was forgiven even before she entered the Pharisee's house. If we pay attention to the Greek phrase we can see the evidence. In verse 37, Luke writes καὶ ἰδοὺ γυνὴ ἥτις ἦν ἐν τῇ πόλει ἁμαρτωλός (and behold! there was a woman in that town who lived a sinful life (NIV)). Luke does not mean, "Now there was a sinful woman in the city" (NAB) but "And a woman in the city who was a sinner" (NRSV). This translation makes a huge difference on how we look at the woman. The position of the phrase "in the city" (ἐν τῇ πόλει) plays an important role to show that her status as a sinner was a past thing but people in the city thought that the woman was still a sinner. They did not notice her change brought about by the Gospel.¹⁷ Moreover the word ἦν

---

¹⁴Bock, *Luke*, 695.
¹⁵Robert H, Stein, *Luke*, (Nashville, TN:B&H Publishing Group, 1992), 236.
¹⁶Bock, *Luke*, 695.
¹⁷Kilgallen, JJ 1998, 'Forgiveness of Sins (Luke 7:36-50)', *Novum Testamentum*, 40, 2, pp. 105-116, ATLA Religion Database with ATLASerials, EBSCOhost, (accessed August 7, 2013).

is an imperfect form and it can be translated as "used to be." She was no longer a sinner even.[18] Also we can see that she was not a sinner anymore from the fact that she brought such expensive perfume to anoint Jesus. Nolland says to that this woman was probably a well-known sinner in the city.[19] Some scholars made a comment that it must have been hard or embarrassing for her to enter such a holy place where only men were eating, and they hated sinners, but I do not agree.[20] She did not really care about those people because her sins were forgiven so she had nothing of which to be ashamed. She went to the Pharisee's house to show how much she appreciated Jesus.

In verse 38, we can see how she showed her gratitude to Jesus. The phrase καὶ στᾶσα ὀπίσω παρὰ τοὺς πόδας αὐτοῦ shows that the woman bravely approached Jesus without considering the rule that the poor or an unwelcomed guest could not get close to the people who were eating. Jesus' sandals were removed before reclining at the table, and his feet were stretched away from the table so she was able to touch them.[21] The things she did were mentioned vividly. These are ἐξέμασσεν, κατεφίλει, and ἤλειφεν. The words wiping, kissing, and anointing are the imperfect tense. They describe the woman's actions as spontaneous and continuous.

When she began to wet Jesus' feet with her tears, Luke uses the word βρέχω. Marshall suggests that this word is used to describe heavy rain.[22] Like rain, this woman shed her tears and wet Jesus' feet. When the woman came to the Pharisee's house, she did not decide to wet Jesus' feet with her tears. What she intended was to anoint Jesus with the perfume, but her crying happened spontaneously. When she approached Jesus, she could not control her emotion anymore because she was so much in love with Jesus. She did not need to live a sinful life anymore. Even though people labeled her as a sinner, she did not need to care about these negative labels and words toward her. She was completely forgiven. She was free! The tears that the woman shed were not artificial or fake but came out from the bottom of her heart.

Her unusual actions were also seen when she used her hair to wipe (ἐξέμασσεν) Jesus' feet. At that time, if a woman untied her hair in public, it meant that she acted like a prostitute to gain favor from men.[23]

---

[18]Reid, B. E. 1995. "'Do You See This Woman?' Luke 7:36-50 as a Paradigm for Feminist Hermeneutics." *Biblical Research* 40, 37-49. New Testament Abstracts, EBSCOhost (accessed August 7, 2013).

[19]John Nolland, *Luke1-9:20*, Word Books Publisher (Dallas, TX, 1989), 9, 353.

[20]Bock, *Luke*, 696.

[21]Leon Morris, *Luke:An Introduction and Commentary*, (Grand Rapids, MI: Wm. B. Eerdmans, 1988), 161.

[22]Marshall, *The Gospel of Luke*, 308.

[23]Green, *The Gospel of Luke*, 310.

We can imagine how much this action of the woman made the guests and the "holy" Pharisee surprised and offended. She was kissing (κατεφίλει) Jesus' feet. This kiss was so intense. The same word κατεφίλεω was used in Luke 15:20 when the lost son came back to his father and in Acts 20:37 when the apostle Paul said farewell to his friends in Ephesus. Finally, she was able to accomplish her original purpose for which she came to the Pharisee's house, anointing (ἤλειφεν) Jesus' feet with the perfume.

Verse 39: Reaction to the Anointing: Doubt about Jesus

Verse 39 shows how the Pharisee judged and labeled Jesus, implying that He was not a prophet. The Pharisee used the word εἰ that means "If" and the following verbs are in the imperfect tense. The Greek word ἅπτεται shows that the Pharisee judged that Jesus was not a prophet by looking at the woman's ongoing action.[24] For the Pharisee, the woman's actions became a test to judge Jesus and, in his eyes, Jesus failed.[25] The word οὗτος means "this man" and it has derogatory meaning.[26] In Jesus' time, like the present time, there was a custom to label people. It has both positive and negative aspects. For example, Jesus was labeled by people as "Christ," "King" (Luke 1:35), "prophet" (Luke 7:16, 39), "teacher" (7:40, 8:49) etc. These are positive labels for Jesus but, at the same time, there are bad labels such as "demon possessed" (11:25), "Polluter," "son of man," etc. Labeling has a strong power if an influential person proclaims that someone is out of his or her social places because of his or her action. Many people, even though they do not know the truth, will follow this influential person's perspective. This labeling can be a weapon to destroy someone's life. At that time, the Pharisees were influential people and if they recognized the woman as a sinner, many would follow them. The Pharisee was not only disappointed by Jesus but also looked down on Him. He thought that Jesus should not have accepted her actions.

At that time, "sinners" were people who did not follow traditional ethics. For example, they were men who hired assassins in pursuit of gain, the men who operated the revenue system from the highest to the lowest, and women who earned their money by prostitution or had been prostitutes. They were not allowed to eat with general and religious people. If someone ate with the sinners, it meant that this person accepted their way of life. So the Pharisee who invited Jesus labeled the

---

[24]Ibid.
[25]David L. Tiede, *Luke* (Minneapolis MN: Augsburg Publishing House, 1988), 161.
[26]Francois Bovon and Helmut Koester, *Luke 1: A Commentary on the Gospel of Luke 1:1-9:50*, trans. Christine M. Thomas, New. (Minneapolis, MN: Fortress Press, 2002), 295.

woman as a sinner who deserved a terrible life and Jesus also joined her. However the fact that Jesus ate with the sinners does not mean that He accepted their way of life, but He knows that this is a great way to show how much He loved them. Jesus ate with them and became their friend in order that the sinners might be saved (5:31, 32; 15:1, 2; 18:14).[27] The Pharisee failed to see this very fact that Jesus came to save sinners. As I have already mentioned, there is a textual issue. Some scribes used the word "the prophet" (ὁ ρροφήτης) instead of using "a prophet" (ρροφήτης) because the scribes wanted to emphasize that the Pharisee's view on Jesus was totally wrong and Jesus was a true prophet like Moses whom the Old Testament promised. Needless to say, even though the scribes use "a prophet", the following verses confirm who Jesus really was. The Pharisee concluded too quickly that Jesus was not a prophet because He did not know what sort of woman was touching Him.

There is a famous saying, "Seeing is believing." Many people see a person's behavior, actions, and speaking and believe that this person is a sinner. This person must live a sinful life. This person does not know how to act as a Christian. However do these people really see the truth? Do they see his or her life story? Do they look into his or her heart? We should not be deceived by this famous saying. Otherwise we might make the same mistake the Pharisee did.

Verse 40-43: Jesus' Reply: A Parable on Forgiveness and Love

In verse 40-43, we can see how Jesus responded to the Pharisee's unspoken complaint by telling the parable about "the two debtors." The Pharisee complained in his mind so nobody but Jesus heard what he said. The phrase ἀροκριθεὶς ὁ Ἰησοῦς εἶρεvvvη ρρὸς αὐτόν is notable. The word ἀροκριθεὶς looks like it is redundant. Luke could simply say "Jesus said" or "Jesus answered." Why did he need to use two words "said" and "answering?" "This usage is most typically found in contexts where there is a change in the direction of the conversation initiated by the new speaker, or the new speaker is about to make an authoritative pronouncement."[28] In verse 39, "Simon said in his mind saying," εἶρεππέν ἑαυτῷ λέγων. There is also a redundancy here. Luke could simply write "Simon said" but Luke did not. But Luke's intention is to put the two phrases ἀροκριθεὶς ὁ Ἰησοῦς εἶρεvvvη ρρὸς αὐτόν and εἶπεν ἐν ἑαυτῷ λέγων as a parallel. It seems like in verse 39, the Pharisee took the initiative by judging that Jesus was not a prophet. In verse 40,

---

[27]J. Duncan M. Derrett, *Jesus' Audience* (London: Darton, Longman & Todd Ltd, 1972), 61–63.

[28]Culy, Parsons, and Stigall, *Luke*, 20.

however, Jesus immediately took back the initiative from the Pharisee answering his challenge by telling a parable.²⁹

The phrase ἔχω σοί τι εἰπεῖρεῖν is a phrase that teachers used with their students to get their attention.³⁰ Jesus also mentioned the name of the Pharisee, Simon, which was a common name in the New Testament. Simon answered Jesus saying διδάσκαλε. The word διδάσκαλον is the title used for Jesus by the crowd (8:49, 9:38, 12:13, 21:7), the religious, the social authorities (10:25, 11:45, 18:18, etc.), or even by Jesus Himself (22:11). So this word was not used in a hostile sense but Bock suggests that if this word is used by someone who doubted Jesus' status or his authority, it could show a tension because in many cases, "The teacher" is used by those who were not Jesus' disciples. The person (Simon) who called Jesus "teacher" did not feel comfortable since he was so disappointed by Jesus' acceptance of the woman.³¹

Jesus told Simon "The parable of two debtors." Whenever the parable is interpreted, one must know the nature of the parable. This parable is a true parable and the hearer, the Pharisee Simon, immediately got Jesus' point. Jesus said that there was a certain moneylender who had two debtors. The one owed five hundred denarii, and the other fifty. δηνάριον (one denarius) is a soldier's or laborer's daily wage, so five hundred denarii indicates one and half year's wage and fifty denarii, two months' wage.³² Jesus continued. Both of the debtors could not pay back their debt so the moneylender cancelled their debt. This very act of the moneylender is unusual. The context where Jesus was speaking was Jewish so one can assume that the two debtors were also Jews. At that time, if a debtor could not pay back money to a moneylender, he would be forgiven in the seventh year (Deut 15) because of the law. At at the same time, however, he could also have been thrown into a prison until the seventh year. So, we can see how merciful the moneylender was.³³ I compared several English translations of verse 42. Most English translations simply say, "The moneylender forgave them both." This translation does not really follow the Greek translation. The word "Forgive" in Greek is χαρίzομαι. In details, it means "Freely forgive." This Greek word was a common business term for remitting debt at that time.³⁴ NASB translates "The moneylender graciously forgave them both." Also, KJV translates in this way, "the moneylender frankly forgave them both." Even though there was no description for "Graciously" in the

---

²⁹Ibid., 278.
³⁰Bovon and Koester, *Luke 1*, 295.
³¹Bock, *Luke*, 698.
³²Ibid.
³³Keener, *The IVP Bible Background Commentary*, 209.
³⁴Bock, *Luke*, 699.

Greek text, I prefer the NASB version that adds the word "graciously." It describes well how special and unusual the moneylender's act was because grace is given to those who do not deserve it. I do not support the KJV translation since it was not easy for the moneylender to forgive the debt. "Graciously" more accurately describes the moneylender's heart.

Briscoe found four points in this parable: we all are sinners in God's debt; we all are responsible for our debt; it is not easy for the moneylender (God) to forgive because he needed to take all the responsibilities; we all need to receive forgiveness by faith.[35] Although some self-righteous people think that their sins are not as bad as some terrible sinners who are around them, everyone is equally a sinner in God's eyes. Jesus told Simon that the one debtor owed fifty denarii but the other one five hundred. The self-righteous think that their debt is only fifty but in God's eyes there is no difference between these two debtors since both of them could not pay him back. Therefore what matters most here is that the woman knew that she was the one who owed five hundred denarii and she knew how gracious the moneylender was, who could cancel all her debt. She admitted her sins but Simon did not. She faced the reality that she could not pay God back, but Simon did not. Jesus said to Simon, "Which of them will love him (the moneylender) more?" The word "will love" in Greek is ἀγαπήσει. It is in the future tense. The tense indicates that the debtor will love the moneylender more after the announcement of forgiveness. It did not happen before the announcement. It shows us that the woman (described as one of the debtors in the parable) was also forgiven before she came to the Pharisee's house. The love of the debtor towards the moneylender involves gratitude. Marshall says that love is the way in which gratitude is expressed. The woman's action shows great love towards Jesus, but this love is based on her gratitude that Jesus had forgiven all her sins. Her expression of her great love had this clear reason.[36]

In verse 42, Jesus asked the Pharisee which debtor will love the moneylender more. Nolland paraphrases Jesus' question in this way, "Don't you recognize in this woman's behavior the love of one who has been forgiven much?"[37] Parables are told to let the hearer reflect on themselves and their actions and respond to the point that is made in the parable. Simon should have responded to Jesus' parable. In verse 43, Simon replied to Jesus, saying "I suppose the one who had the bigger debt forgiven." (NIV) The phrase "I suppose" in Greek is υjρολαμβάνω.

---

[35]D. Stuart Briscoe, *Patterns for Power* (Delight, AR: Gospel Light Publications, 1979), 12–17.
[36]Marshall, *The Gospel of Luke*, 311.
[37]Nolland, *Luke1-9:20*, 359.

One question comes up here. Jesus' parable was easy to comprehend. His point was obvious to everyone who heard the story of the two-debtors, but why did Simon answer, "I suppose . . . ?" The Greek word suggests, "To regard something as presumably true, but without particular certainty."[38] The most natural conclusion is that Simon knew the right answer but he pretended that he had no confidence in his answer because a trap caught him. Simon totally got Jesus' point. Notice Jesus' indirect accusation, "Don't you recognize in this woman's behavior the love of one who has been forgiven much?" Jesus accused him of having a self-righteous attitude and a lack of gratitude and love. The Pharisees did not want to admit it. Bock suggests that Simon was also careful to answer Jesus' question because Jesus' response towards his unspoken complaint was quick and sharp. He did not want to be trapped again.[39]

In Part I of this article, the relationship of the Lukan passage to the same passages in the other Synoptic Gospels, a translation of the passage and a textual criticism have been presented in addition to the exegesis of 7:36-43. Part II will present the remainder of my exegesis from 7:44-50, conclusions and applications.

---

[38]Culy, Parsons, and Stigall, *Luke*, 247.
[39]Bock, *Luke*, 700.

Is She a Sinful Woman or a Forgiven Woman?
An Exegesis of Luke 7:36-50
Part II

By Yuri Phanon

Exegesis of Luke 7:44-50

Verses 44-46: The Woman's Acts of Love Defended

In verses 44-46, Jesus started defending the woman's action. By hearing the parable of the two debtors, Simon the Pharisee may have gotten Jesus' main point that the woman's great love was a product of the great forgiveness, but Jesus gave Simon more details by comparing their actions. Verse 44 starts with the phrase καὶ στραφεὶς ππὸς τὴν γυναῖκα. The word στραφεὶς has the function of bringing the woman back to the center of this narrative. The word "See" in Greek in this verse is βλέπεις. This word is used in the Gospel of Luke many times and is used as a metaphor for perceiving the word of God. In Luke, to see the truth is to perceive the word of God.[1] There are two kinds of people in view here, one who receives the word of God and the other who does not receive it. For example, in Luke 2:20, after the shepherds saw baby Jesus, they rejoiced and praised God for all they had heard and seen. They are an example of seeing God's truth. On the other hand, Herod wanted to see Jesus but he did not believe in him. The Gospel of Luke used this comparison a lot and one of them is seen here in 7:44. Jesus asked Simon, "Do you see?" This word is not merely to ask Simon to see what the woman did but to see God's truth that she was a woman who was forgiven by God and showed much greater love than Simon did.[2] As I mentioned in Part I, Simon failed to see it. Jesus started to retell what the woman did for Jesus in order to make a vivid contrast between Simon and the woman, and He mentioned three things: water, kiss, and oil (ὕδωρ, φίλημά, ἐλαίῳ). The first thing Jesus mentioned was water. The structure of the entire sentence εἰσῆλθόν σου εἰς τὴν οἰκίαν, ὕδωρ μοι ἐπὶ πόδας οὐκ ἔδωκας, is important to note. The word ὕδωρ is a direct object of ἔδωκας. Elsewhere in the Gospel of Luke, there are 167 examples of a verb with two complements following it. However in only four other places in Luke do the two complements precede the

---

[1]Reid, B. E. 1995. "'Do You See This Woman?' Luke 7:36-50 as a Paradigm for Feminist Hermeneutics." *Biblical Research* 40, 37-49. New Testament Abstracts, EBSCOhost (accessed August 7, 2013).
[2]Ibid.

verb. Three of them are seen here in verse 44, 45, and 46.³ Two complements ὕδωρ μοι precede the verb ἔδωκας. This structure shows the speaker's emphasis on the word that comes first. The three things that Jesus mentioned, ὕδωρ, φίλημά, ἐλαίῳ, to compare Simon and the woman's action are parallel and do not have a conjunction.

Providing water (ὕδωρ) for a guest, although not necessarily required, showed warm hospitality. At that time, people wore sandals so their feet were usually dirty. To provide water made the guest feel relaxed and comfortable. Simon did not give the water to Jesus, but the woman wet Jesus' feet with her tears and wiped them with her hair. In verse 45, Jesus mentioned a kiss (φίλημά). A kiss was a friendly greeting but was not really necessary to give to a guest. However the woman could not stop kissing Jesus' feet. That they may have been dirty made no difference to her. In verse 46, Jesus mentioned olive oil (ἐλαίῳ). This olive oil was not expensive, but Simon the Pharisee did not anoint Jesus' feet with anything. Simon did not provide water, give a kiss, or anoint Jesus, but the woman did all these things. Green suggests that her actions should be seen as more than a substitute for Simon's lack of hospitality. Like Simon, she did not provide water, but she washed Jesus' feet with her tears that were more valuable than water in Jesus' eyes. She did not wipe Jesus' feet with a clean towel, but she wiped them with her hair. She did not kiss Jesus' cheek or hand that was a typical Jewish custom at that time, but kissed Jesus' feet as a sign of humility. She did more than Simon did because she loved Jesus much and was grateful for what Jesus had done in her life. We cannot judge that Simon was so rude to Jesus because he did not provide these three things, but we can say that he did not warmly welcome Jesus. In Jesus' eyes, her unnatural actions became natural. The role of host (Simon) and intruder are interchanged. Her actions were considered to be strange by Simon and other dinner guests. Even some of them thought that her attitude was like a prostitute, but in Jesus' eyes, her warm welcome was natural for a forgiven sinner and Simon's welcome as a host became unnatural.⁴

Verse 47: Much Forgiveness in Contrast to Little

Jesus said, οὗ χάριν, λέγω σοι, ἀφέωνται αἱ ἁμαρτίαι αὐτῆς αἱ πολλαί, ὅτι ἠγάπησεν πολύ· ᾧ δὲ ὀλίγον ἀφίεται, ὀλίγον ἀγαπᾷ. (Therefore, I tell you, her many sins have been forgiven as her great love has shown. But whoever has been forgiven little loves little (NIV)). Jesus concluded his teaching saying "therefore" (οὗ χάριν). There is an argument among scholars about which phrase "I tell you" (λέγω σοι) or "her many sins have been forgiven" (ἀφέωνται αἱ ἁμαρτίαι αὐτῆς αἱ πολλαί) receives the word "therefore" (οὗ χάριν). It seems a minor and unimportant argument, but depending on which phrase receives

---

³Martin M. Culy, Mikeal Carl Parsons, and Joshua J. Stigall, *Luke: A Handbook on the Greek Text* (Waco, TX: Baylor University Press, 2010), 248.

⁴Resseguie, James L. 1992. "Luke 7:36-50." *Interpretation* 46, no. 3: 285-290. ATLA Religion Database with ATLASerials, EBSCOhost (accessed August 7, 2013).

"therefore" (οὗ χάριν), or it will totally change the theology of forgiveness. If we take the position that supports "I tell you" (λέγω σοι) as a receiver of "therefore" (οὗ χάριν), we can translate the entire sentence this way. "Therefore (because of this conduct), I tell you that her many sins have been forgiven, as is evidenced by the fact that she loved much."[5] On the other hand, if we take the other position, the translation of the whole sentence will be like this: "I tell you. Therefore her many sins have been forgiven because she loved much." We see that these two translations have a significant difference. The first translation shows that her great love was based on forgiveness she received before entering the Pharisee's house, but the other translation shows that because of her love and actions such as wiping, kissing, and anointing, her sins were forgiven. Besides, how to translate word ὅτι is as important as the previous issue. Many times, this word is translated as "for" or "because." So we tend to translate ὅτι here in verse 47 the same. However it should not be understood as a causal sense but as a content conjunction.[6] So, like Marshall, it is proper to translate ὅτι as "as is evidenced."

Furthermore, we should also take a look at the word ἀφέωνται. Since this word is in the perfect tense, here we can see another piece of evidence that the woman's forgiveness occurred before that time. The passive form is also important because it tells us that God was the one who has given the forgiveness.[7]

All in all, I support the view that the woman's love was a result of God's forgiveness; not because she showed love, she was forgiven. Some English translations do not show this truth. For example, NASB translates in this way, "For this reason I say to you, her sins which are many have been forgiven for she loved much; but he who is forgiven little, loves little." The NRSV translates, "Therefore, I tell you, her sins, which were many, have been forgiven; hence she has shown great love. But the one to whom little is forgiven, loves little." I think this kind of translation will cause confusion among the readers especially those who are new Christians. I prefer how the GNB and the TNIV translate the passage. The GNB says, "the great love she has shown proves that her many sins have been forgiven" The NIV says, "her many sins have been forgiven- as her great love has shown" These two are excellent translations that do not make the readers misunderstand that the forgiveness is based on love.

For the second half of verse 47, the NIV translation is not correct, "But he who has been forgiven little loves little" (NIV). The word ἀφίεται is the present tense so we should not translate this in a perfect tense since Luke intentionally made a difference here. In Greek, if a statement is described in the present tense that means that it is a general statement. So here Jesus told a general truth that

---

[5] I. Howard Marshall, *The Gospel of Luke: A Commentary on the Greek Text* (Kingstown, Broadway: Paternoster Press, 1978), 313.

[6] Max Zerwick, *A Grammatical Analysis of the Greek New Testament* (Piazza della Pilotta: Roma: Editrice Pontificio Istituto Biblico, 1996), 203.

[7] Barbara E. Reid, *Choosing the Better Part?: Women in the Gospel of Luke* (Collegeville, Minn: Michael Glazier, 1996), 114.

the one who is forgiven little loves little. If we translate this passage in the perfect tense, we miss the point that Luke was not pointing out Simon personally. It cannot be a precise application to Simon since he did not believe in Jesus and the teaching of John the Baptist.[8] He did not acknowledge Jesus as Savior or a prophet. Simon had not even reached a standard Jesus made here "the one who is forgiven little loves little." He was not yet forgiven at this point.

The one who is forgiven little loves little. Everyone is equally a sinner before God but not everyone recognizes that they need forgiveness, great forgiveness. This makes a huge difference in how we live our Christian life. We can live as if we are not great sinners by judging others, but it is so shameful to do so.

Verse 48: Jesus' Response: Forgiveness Extended
to the Woman

"Then Jesus said to her, Ἀφέωνταί σου αἱ ἁμαρτίαι. Even though the woman knew that she was forgiven, Jesus announced it in public. The word ἀφέωνται is already seen in verse 47. As I have already explained above, a perfect tense explains a thing that has already taken place. The woman was forgiven, so why did Jesus still need to make an announcement? According to Bock, Jesus intentionally said it in public to confuse the dinner guests. Bock claims that if Jesus did not make the public comment they could have thought that the woman's actions were either honorable or offensive. However, the guests, Bock alleges, were offended by the fact that Jesus publicly claimed to have the authority to forgive the woman when that authority, they believed, only came from God.[9] Marshall and some other commentators say that the reason that Jesus made an announcement was to give the woman a personal assurance, but I do not agree with this view.[10]

Luke had a special intention of writing Jesus' proclamation of the forgiveness, because forgiveness is one of the major theological themes in his Gospel. For example, in 1:77, Zachariah says that John the Baptist came to give the people the knowledge of salvation through the forgiveness of sins. Also in 6:37, Jesus himself says, "Forgive and you will be forgiven," and in 17:3, "If your brother sins, rebuke him, and if he repents, forgive him." In 23:34, "Forgive them Father, for they know not what they do." In his very last words before Jesus left the world, he said, "Repentance and forgiveness of sins will be preached in his name to all nations" (24:47). As already noted, forgiveness is one of the central themes of the Gospel of Luke. Apparently, Luke wanted to emphasize the fact that salvation comes through the forgiveness of sins.[11]

---

[8]John Nolland, *Luke 1-9:20*, Word Books Publisher (Dallas, TX, 1989), 358.
[9]Darrell Bock, *Luke: 1:1-9:50*, (Ada, MI: Baker Books, 1994), 705.
[10]Marshall, *The Gospel of Luke*, 314.
[11]Van Til, K. A. 2006. "Three Anointings and One Offering: The Sinful Woman in Luke 7.36-50." *Journal Of Pentecostal Theology* 15, no. 1: 73-82. New Testament Abstracts, EBSCOhost (accessed August 7, 2013), 76.

Verse 49: The Pharisees' Reaction: Who Is This?

"The other guests began to say among themselves, 'Who is this who even forgives sins?'" (NIV) This verse deals with a matter of Jesus' identity. "Who is Jesus?" This question frequently arises throughout the Gospel of Luke. This major concern is seen in Luke in chapters 7, 8, 9, and 22. As I have mentioned above we can also see that forgiveness is one of major terms in Luke's work (Luke 5:21, 24:47, Acts 10:43, 17:30). Bock suggests that the reason that Luke wrote a lot about forgiveness was that he wanted to show his readers that to be saved, it is necessary to recognize Jesus' authority to forgive sins. Everyone who is seeking the truth must go through this process.[12]

Jesus' proclamation of the forgiveness for the woman was not for personal assurance for her but for the other dinner guests. His word caused great confusion among them. Simon's reaction in this verse is not known. It does not say if Simon responded to Jesus' parable and had a heart to repent and admit that Jesus was a prophet. However, at least the other dinner guests were greatly offended. Why? In their eyes, Jesus acted like God himself who only can forgive one's sins.[13] This was the normal reaction for those who strictly observed the Jewish law. The Pharisees believed that as long as they gave the offering at the temple, their sins would be forgiven so it was unbearable for them to see that Jesus had such authority besides God.

The phrase ἐν ἑαυτοῖς suggests that it is possible that the other dinner guests showed their confusion and complaints verbally. They said, Τίς οὗτός ἐστιν ὃς καὶ ἁμαρτίας ἀφίησιν. The word ἀφίησιν is in the present tense. It shows that the dinner guests felt that Jesus' active declaring of forgiveness as the judge declares, "This person is not guilty" at the court. If Jesus said in verse 47, "God has forgiven your sins" instead of saying "Your sins have been forgiven," the Pharisees would not have a problem with Jesus. However since Jesus said, Ἀφέωνταί σου αἱ ἁμαρτίαι, they had a problem with this phrase. The word "forgive" here is passive. Stein named this passive usage "divine passive" to show Jesus' authority.[14] In spite of the dinner guests' arguments, Jesus did not give an answer. Luke wanted his readers to have their own decision and it is so clear who Jesus is in the context of this passage.[15]

Verse 50: Jesus' Confirmation: The Woman's Faith Has Saved Her

The dinner guests might have recognized that Jesus was a prophet but verse 50 clearly tells us that Jesus is more than a prophet. This is the main point of this verse. One of the roles of the prophets in the Old Testament was to proclaim

---

[12]Bock, *Luke*, 706–707.
[13]Joel B. Green, *The Gospel of Luke*, (Grand Rapids, MI: Wm. B. Eerdmans, 1997), 314.
[14]Stein, *Luke*, 238.
[15]Marshall, *The Gospel of Luke*, 314.

God's Word. As we read through the Old Testament, we see their typical sayings "the Lord says" or "The Lord will forgive." The prophets were not God himself but they were the mouthpieces of God. On the other hand, Jesus' proclamation of forgiveness in verse 48, (Ἀφέωνταί σου αἱ ἁμαρτίαι) over the woman did not have "The Lord says" since Jesus is the Lord himself and has authority to do it. Jesus said, "I tell you." This phrase is exactly opposite to the prophet's declaration, "The Lord says," in the Old Testament.

Once again, Jesus declared, ἡ πίστις σου σέσωκέν σε. The word σέσωκέν is in the perfect tense; she was not only forgiven but was saved. What made it possible was her πίστις. She had never heard a direct word of forgiveness until that time, but she was able to believe that she was forgiven and saved. The woman's πίστις was the faith that did not wait for the word of forgiveness or did not simply come to Jesus to ask for His help but to respond to what had already taken place (forgiveness), grabbed it for herself and showed gratitude for it. Noland describes her faith in this way, "Faith is seen when there is no break in the pattern of divine initiative and human response by means of which a restored relationship to God is established."[16] Faith should include a human response and without it we cannot call it genuine "faith." In the Gospel of Luke, we can see this pattern in 8:43-48 and 12:12-19. Having faith means there should not be doubt. If she had a little doubt that she was really was forgiven, she might have gone to the Pharisee's house to receive a confirmation from Jesus. However she did not. She went there with gratitude that shows that there was no doubt in her heart. Rather she was full of joy, love and gratitude.

Right after Jesus said, "Your faith has saved you," he continued, πορεύου εἰς εἰρήνην. This phrase is a common farewell formula in Judaism. Hendricksen says this phrase shows "prosperity for both soul and body," can be meant here. This peace is the smile of God reflected in the heart of the redeemed sinner, a shelter in the storm, a hiding-place in the cleft of the rock, and under his wings."[17]

To sum up, we can see the principle in this episode. In verse 48, Jesus said, "Your sins have been forgiven" but now "Your faith has saved you." What is the connection between two phrases? Bovon explains well. "Love for Jesus and forgiveness are now expressed with different words, as "faith" and "salvation." Luke uses these concepts interchangeably."[18] I would like to add the word "peace" (εἰρήνη). If there is salvation, there should be faith, love, forgiveness, and peace. If there is forgiveness, there should be salvation, love, faith, and peace. These four concepts go together and should not be separated. There was a message of Jesus who proclaimed that God's kingdom had come and He was sent by God to save the sinners. Somewhere, the woman heard this message of salvation and forgiveness. She received it with faith, was saved and had great

---

[16]Nolland, *Luke1-9:20*, 360.

[17]William Hendriksen, *Exposition of the Gospel According to Luke*, (Grand Rapids, MI: Baker Book House, 1978), 410.

[18]Francois Bovon and Helmut Koester, *Luke 1:A Commentary on the Gospel of Luke 1:1-9:50*.Translated by Christine M. Thomas. New. (Minneapolis, MN: Fortress Press, 1979), 298.

gratitude and love. She was looked down on by most of the people in the city. People did not know how much she was grateful, how much she was changed. However it does not matter for her for she had peace in her heart. Jesus sent the woman in peace so she would live in peace whatever situations would surround her in the future.

Application

This section will discuss applications that can be made from what has been learned in the exegesis of Luke 7:36-50.

Christians Should Show Extraordinary Love Because They Have Been Forgiven Greatly

The woman showed extraordinary love because she was forgiven greatly. The more she was forgiven, the more she loved Jesus. Since every single person on the earth is a sinner, there is no difference among them. No one can say, "This guy's sins are less than that guy's sins." So what matters most is how one sees and understands the meaning of forgiveness. If their understanding of forgiveness is not enough, their love will never grow, just like the Pharisee. The woman understood the meaning of forgiveness well, so she responded well. Thus, one's knowledge and love of God and people are not enough. People's love does not always respond well to God's forgiveness. At that time, perhaps the woman did not know what Jesus was going to do in the future. Jesus would be crucified on the cross to forgive all the sins in the world. However, still, she understood the meaning of forgiveness better than many Christians who know the history of salvation more than she did.

Is It Important How People Look At Christians?

If someone asks a Christian, "Is it important how people look at you?" that person should definitely say, "No." What matters is how God looks at someone. However, even if a Christian responds in this manner, it does not mean that he or she live out this truth. People have different perspectives on individuals and, therefore, no one can control how they are viewed. If someone paid attention too much to words and rumors about themselves, they would never know who they really were. This could cause that person to not be themselves. The Pharisee and most of the people in the city saw the woman as an unclean sinner who did not deserve God's grace and forgiveness. She was dirty in people's eyes. Yes, she used to be a sinner but for them, she was always a sinner. They never looked at the change in her that was caused by the Gospel and the fact that they too needed God's forgiveness. However, did the woman care how people looked at her? Apparently not. Many Christians pay attention too much to how people look at them even though God has already forgiven them and cleansed all their sins. Instead, Christians should be prepared to go into the house of the Pharisee simply to search for what they can do to show their gratitude for what God has done in their life instead of crying with despair because of how people look at them.

Don't Label, Don't Judge: Don't Be Like The Pharisee

Labeling and Judging are part of human nature and are sinful. It is surprising to see how people are quick to label and judge others. Sometimes people act like Simon the Pharisee who labeled the woman as a great sinner. But the Pharisee did not see that he too was a sinner. This kind of sinful and evil habit can cause people to be quick to judge and label others. However, one should always remember the phrase, "Both of them are not able to pay back their debt." Do not want to be like the Pharisee but rather be like Jesus who had eyes that were full of love and compassion. Amy Carmichael says in her book, *If: What Do I Know of Calvary Love?*, "If I belittle those whom I am called to serve, talk of their weak points in contrast perhaps with what I think of as my strong points; if I adopt a superior attitude, forgetting 'Who made thee to differ?' and 'What has thou that thou hast not received?' then I know nothing of Calvary love."[19]

Conclusion

In the story of the sinful woman who anointed Jesus (Luke 7:36-50), Jesus makes a point about love and forgiveness. As has been discussed in this paper, his statement on this matter has been the subject of debate among scholars and pastors. The heart of the issue deals with Jesus' perspective on the relationship between love and forgiveness. Was the woman forgiven because she loved much? Or did she love much because she was forgiven?

In this paper, I have presented a detailed exegesis of this passage, including a discussion of textual criticism, in order to clarify this issue. From this study, I have concluded that the sinful woman in this passage loved much because she had already been forgiven by Jesus. This conclusion is contrary to the misinterpretation of some who believe the converse; that Jesus forgave the woman because she loved much.

The following is a summary of the evidence that the woman was forgiven before she entered the Pharisee's house.

The first evidence (see verse 37) is seen in the Greek phrase γυνὴ ἥτις ἦν ἐν τῇ πόλει ἁμαρτωλός. The translation should be "There was a woman who used to be a sinner in the city." The word "in the city" (ἐν τῇ πόλει) between "a certain woman was" (γυνὴ ἥτις ἦν) and "a sinner" (ἁμαρτωλός) is important. It means she was considered to be a sinner by the people in the city despite the fact that was no longer a sinner. Also the word ἦν is the imperfect tense. Again, it shows that she was no longer a sinner.

---

[19] Amy Carmichael, *If: What Do I Know of Calvary Love?* (Fort Washington, PA: CLC Publications, 2011), 13.

The second evidence (see verse 38) is seen in her actions that she brought some expensive perfume to anoint Jesus' feet. Along with all her actions such as crying, wiping, kissing and anointing, this clearly showed that all these actions were products of great forgiveness that she received from God.

The third evidence (see verse 41) is seen in Jesus' interaction with Simon the Pharisee. After Jesus told Simon the parable of the two debtors, Jesus asked a question, "Now, which of them will love him (the moneylender) more?" In Greek, "he will love" is ἀγαρήσει. The debtor who was forgiven more refers to the woman and this debtor will love the moneylender after he received the announcement of being debt-free. The woman's great love being shown to Jesus happened after she received forgiveness from God.

The fourth evidence is seen in verse 47. Careful observation of the words οὗ χάριν, ὅτι, and ἀφέωνται is the key to understand the principle of forgiveness. The word οὗ χάριν is received by the phrase λέγω σοι. Moreover, ὅτι should be translated as a content conjunction, so the translation is not "because" or "for," but "as is evidenced by." Also, it is important to note that ἀφέωνται is the perfect tense.

To sum up, the translation of verse 47 will be like this; "Therefore, I tell you that her many sins have been forgiven, as is evidenced by the fact that she loved much." It is obvious that forgiveness happened before the woman came to the Pharisee's house.

The fifth evidence is seen in the last verse when Jesus told the woman, Ἡ ρίστις σου σέσωκέν σε. The tense is the perfect tense. Her salvation and forgiveness occurred when she accepted the message of salvation before she came to the Pharisee's house. It did not happen when she met Jesus face to face in the house.

By looking at these five pieces of evidence and apply the theology of forgiveness we can say with confidence that we love God because He loves us first and forgives us. Not, he loves us and forgives us because we love him first. Many times preachers and ministers tend to misunderstand this basic principle as they preach on this passage. Preachers misunderstand that the woman's actions are not a product of love but that of repentance. All of these are wrong interpretations and the messages of the Gospel do not include these false teachings. Ministers should always pay attention to God's truth that God loves us first. Every minister knows this simple statement, but sometimes we misinterpret the Bible and create false teaching and proclaim it without noticing. This is our responsibility as leaders, preachers and students of the word of God.

Bibliography

Aland, Kurt. *Synopsis of the Four Gospels: Completely Revised on the Basis of the Greek Text of the Nestle-Aland 26th Edition and Greek New Testament 3rd Edition* : the Text Is the Second Edition of the Revised Standard Version. United Bible Societies, 1985.

Barclay, William. *The Gospel of Luke*. Louisville, KY: Westminster John Knox Press, 2001.

Bock, Darrell L. *Luke: 1:1-9:50*. Ada, MI: Baker Books, 1994.

Bovon, Francois, and Helmut Koester. *Luke 1: A Commentary on the Gospel of Luke 1:1-9:50*. Translated by Christine M. Thomas. New. Minneapolis, MN: Fortress Press, 2002.

Briscoe, D. Stuart. *Patterns for Power*. Delight, AR: Gospel Light Publications, 1979.

Carmichael, Amy. *If: What Do I Know of Calvary Love?* Fort Washington, PA: CLC Publications, 2011.

Cosgrove, C. H. "A Woman's Unbound Hair in the Greco-Roman World, with Special Reference to the Story of the 'Sinful Woman' in Luke 7:36-50." *Journal Of Biblical Literature* 124, no.4 2005): 675-692. New Testament Abstracts, EBSCOhost (accessed August 7, 2013).

Culy, Martin M., Mikeal, Carl Parsons, and Joshua J. Stingall. *Luke: A Hand book on the Greek Text*. Waco, TX: Baylor University Press, 2010.

English, Jennifer A. "Which Woman? Reimagining the Woman Who Anoints Jesus in Luke 7:36-50." *Currents In Theology And Mission* 39, no. 6 (December 1, 2012): 435-441. ATLA Religion Database with ATLASerials, EBSCOhost (accessed August 7, 2013).

Evans, Craig A. *Luke (Understanding the Bible Commentary Series)*. Grand Rapids, MI: Baker Books, 1990.

Derrett, J. Duncan M. *Jesus' Audience*. London: Darton,Longman & Todd Ltd, 1972.

Fee, Gordon D., and Douglas Stuart. *How to Read the Bible for All Its Worth*: Fourth Edition. Grand Rapids, MI: Zondervan, 2014.

Fitzmyer, Joseph. *The Gospel According to Luke I-IX*. Broadway, NY: Doubleday Religious Publishing Group, 1995.

Gooding, David. *According to Luke: A New Exposition of the Third Gospel*. Downers Grove, IL: Inter-Varsity Press, 1987.

Green, Joel B. *The Gospel of Luke*. Grand Rapids, MI: Wm. B. Eerdmans Publishing, 1997.

Hendriksen, William. *Exposition of the Gospel According to Luke*. Grand Rapids, MI: Baker Book House, 1978.

James, Resseguie L. "Luke 7:36-50." *Interpretation* 46, no. 3: (1992): 285-290. ATLA Religion Database with ATLASerials, EBSCOhost (accessed August 7, 2013).

Keener, Craig S. *The IVP Bible Background Commentary: New Testament*. Downers Grove, IL: InterVarsity Press, 1993.

Kilgallen, J. J. "Forgiveness of Sins (Luke 7:36-50)." *Novum Testamentum* 40, no. 2 (1998): 105-116. New Testament Abstracts, EBSCOhost (accessed August 7, 2013).

Kilgallen, J. J. "John the Baptist, the Sinful Woman, and the Pharisee." *Journal Of Biblical Literature* 104, no. 4 (1985): 675-679. New Testament Abstracts, EBSCOhost (accessed August 7, 2013).

Kitzberger, I. R. "Love and Footwashing : John 13:1-20 and Luke 7:36-50 Read Intertextually." *Biblical Interpretation* 2, no. 2 (1994): 190-206. New Testament Abstracts, EBSCOhost (accessed August 7, 2013).

Ladd, George Eldon. *A Theology of the New Testament*. Grand Rapids, MI: William. B. Eerdmans Publishing, 1993.

Lewis, C. S. *A Mind Awake: An Anthology of C. S. Lewis*. Boston, MA: Houghton Mifflin Harcourt, 2003.

McKnight, Scot. *Interpreting the Synoptic Gospels (Guides to New Testament Exegesis)*. Ada, MI: Baker Books, 1988.

Marshall, I. Howard. *The Gospel of Luke: A Commentary on the Greek Text*. Kingstown, Broadway: Paternoster Press, 1978.

Morris, Leon. *Luke: An Introduction and Commentary*. Grand Rapids, MI: Wm. B. Eerdmans Publishing, 1988.

Nickle, Keith Fullerton. *The Synoptic Gospels: An Introduction*. Louisville, KY: Westminster John Knox Press, 2001.

Nolland, John. *Luke1-9:20*. Word Books Publisher. Dallas, TX, 1989.

Omanson, Roger L. *A Textual Guide to the Greek New Testament: An Adaptation of Bruce M. Metzger's Textual Commentary for the Needs of Translators*. Stuttgart: Deutsche Bibelgesellschaf, 2007.

Reid, Barbara E. *Choosing the Better Part?: Women in the Gospel of Luke.* New. Collegeville, Minn: Michael Glazier, 1996.

Reid, B. E. "'Do You See This Woman?' Luke 7:36-50 as a Paradigm for Feminist Hermeneutics.*Biblical Research* 40, (1995): 37-49. New Testament Abstracts, EBSCOhost (accessed August 7, 2013).

Stein, Robert H. *Luke*. Nashville, TN: B&H Publishing Group, 1992.

Tiede, David L. *Luke*. Minneapolis MN: Augsburg Publishing House, 1988.

Yancey, Philip. *The Jesus I Never Knew*. Grand Rapids, MI: Zondervan, 1996.

Book Review 85

Richard Averbeck et al., *Reading Genesis 1-2: An Evangelical Conversation*, ed. J. Daryl Charles (Massachusetts: Hendrickson Publishers, 2013). xiv + 240pp. $14.98.

This book is the result of a symposium which was held at Bryan College, 2011 with seven Old Testament (OT) scholars, namely Richard E. Averbeck (Professor of Trinity Evangelical Divinity School), Todd S. Beall (Professor of Capital Bible Seminary), John Collins (a professor of Covenant Theological Seminary), Tremper Longman III (a professor of Westmont College), John H. Walton (a professor of Wheaton College and the Wheaton Graduate School), Kenneth J. Turner (a professor of Bryan College), and Jud Davis (a Greek professor of Bryan College).

There is no doubt that there have been many debates regarding the interpretation and meaning of Genesis 1-2 among scholars. As the title indicates, this book aims to demonstrate the hermeneutical diversity of Genesis 1-2.

Part I presents five different views on interpreting Genesis 1-2. Part 2 deals with pedagogical format with the creation account in Genesis 1 in terms of modern discussions (chapter 6) and seven barriers which prevent the readers from joining the current evangelical majority as the reflection of symposium (chapter 7).

In chapter 1, Richard E. Averbeck deals with three purposes: a literary day, inter-textual and contextual issues. Regarding literary features of Genesis 1-2, he mentions *vav consecutive* (and/then) which serves to express actions or events which are to be regarded as logical sequel of preceding actions or events. He explains days of creation from day 1 to day 6 in relation to *vav consecutive* which is the first word of each day and begins a common Hebrew account: circumstantial information with action; for example, "and/then God said." Unlike this formula, he ascertains that Genesis 1:1 should be understood as an independent clause which is the title of the book because it does not begin with *vav consecutive* and it just provides the readers with the first glimpse of the whole creation account. He believes that there is a common literary pattern in each day of creation such as divine decree, a narrative description of the fulfillment of the decree, and an evening and morning formula. Furthermore, he says that the seven days should be understood as the cosmic framework in which we live although they are not to be taken literally.

Aside from much commendation for his essay, I am very satisfied with his uses of Ancient Near East (ANE) materials. He is well balanced in terms of the handling of ANE texts. While he finds helpful and significant parallels of ANE texts with the biblical texts, he does not neglect to mention the contrasts among them.

In chapter 2, unlike the shift in evangelical scholarship over the past twenty years from a literal understanding of Genesis 1-11, (especially Genesis 1-2) to a figurative reading, Beall insists that the literal approach to these chapters is the correct approach. In other words, he ascertains that Genesis 1-2 as well as

Genesis 1-11 should be taken as a literal, historical account, just like Jesus and the New Testament writers did. For this matter, he presents five key questions regarding different hermeneutics for Genesis-11 and Gen 12-50, a separate hermeneutic or genre for Genesis 1, Genesis 1 as representing an ANE worldview, the New Testament writers' approach to Gen 1-11, and recent non-literal views motivated by current scientific theories.

One of the interesting issues is that the New Testament passages referring to Genesis 1-11 were used literally, such as 2 Corinthians 11:3 (account of the fall in Genesis 3), John 3:12, Luke 11:51 and Matt 23:35 (Cain's murder of Abel in Genesis 4), Matthew 24:37-38 (account of the flood in Genesis 6-8), and so on.

I agree with the author's understanding that Genesis 1-11 should not be separated from the remaining chapters in terms of genres. Wehnham's treatment of Genesis 1 as a hymn is not the proper way. As Beall mentions, we can easily recognize that the doxology of hymns known to the ANE is absent. Furthermore, Genesis 1 uses *vav* consecutive which is the standard form of Hebrew normal narrative fifty times in Genesis 1. In the same way, the starting word of Genesis 12 is *wayyomer*, which means "and he said."

In chapter 3, C. John Collins explains that we should read Genesis 1-2 for what it aims to say and do. In other words, he ascertains that we should approach Genesis 1-2 based on its context, to whom it was written, and for what purpose. He believes that Genesis 2 elaborates on the events of the sixth day of Genesis 1 rather than being a second, separate creation account. In addition, he insists that Genesis 1-2 should be treated as a preface for the rest of Genesis. In this way, the difference in style between Genesis 1 and 2 can be understood as complementary rather than contradictory. Furthermore, he believes that Genesis 1-2 and Genesis 1-11 need to be read as part of a coherent whole.

Personally, I am not persuaded by his argument that Genesis 1-2 needs to be read as a preface of the book, which comes before the ordinary historical narrative. It is the account of creation which uses the normal marker for narrative such as the fifty occurrences of *vav* consecutive in Genesis 1. In this matter, to treat Genesis 1-2 as a preface of the book is not reasonable and understandable.

In chapter 4, Tremper Longman III tries to present what Genesis 1-2 teaches us. He ascertains that the main goal of Genesis 1-2 is to proclaim that God is the real creator among other contemporary gods. Genesis 1-2 should be read as the device which helps the readers to know that God is the Creator as opposed to any other god, and the Bible is not interested in describing how God did it at all. He insists that the genre of a passage is one of the most significant things for proper interpretation. He classifies Genesis 1-2 as theological history which conveys figurative narrative. The major point of his article is to present the teachings that readers should find from reading Genesis 1-2 in terms of God, humanity, and the world. These teachings include: God who created creation is the Lord God, the God of Moses, and God of Israel who is sovereign and supreme; the creator God of Genesis is not gendered like other gods of nations;

and humans have a special relationship with God because they are a part of creation.

One of his strong arguments is to understand that the ANE plays important roles when we see Genesis 1 and 2 in terms of comparison and contrast. For instance, his elucidation of the Babylonian account of creation involves contrast as well as comparison with the biblical account. Both mention similar components such as earth, breath, blood, and spit from the divine. However, he did not neglect to highlight the different view of humanity: a low view by the Babylonian account, but a dignified picture by the biblical account.

However, his understanding about the genre of Genesis 1-2 is not clear enough. From the beginning of his article, he emphasizes that the description regarding creation of the world and of humanity in chapters 1-2 should be read as figurative language which is not literally true. Finally he arrives at "theological history" as its fine genre. Unfortunately, he does not define what he means by the term "theological history." Definitely, it brings his readers into confusion.

In chapter 5, John H. Walton argues that we have to be competent and ethical readers. By competent, he means the Bible should be read in the light of the culture in which it was conveyed. On the other hand, by ethical, he means we need to embrace Bible teachings as valid and agree with the text and be instructed by it. He suggests that we read the first chapters of Genesis as cosmology whose central intention is to provide an elucidation of the cosmos. In order for the readers to understand Genesis 1-2 in a proper way, he insists that we have to know ANE cosmology. For this purpose, he ascertains first that we read the text competently based on literary genre as well as its ANE context, second, that we have to read the text ethically according to what it intends to teach the readers and third, that we need to read the Bible virtuously as it was intended to challenge both ancient and modern readers.

Having read his article, I recognize that it is helpful and significant in terms of its uses of ANE materials for Old Testament studies. However, it seems he puts too much focus on ANE materials rather than the OT text itself for its interpretation. Though it is true to say that we need to investigate the surrounding materials for the information of its culture and custom, it is more significant to depend upon other OT texts first as long as we are talking about OT interpretation.

This book is helpful for those who want to understand more thoroughly the variety of ways of interpreting Genesis 1-2. Definitely, its various interpretations will broaden the perspectives of its readers.

David Im Seok Kang

Chas. H. Barfoot, *Aimee Semple McPherson and the Making of Modern Pentecostalism 1890-1926* (London, UK & Oakville, CT: Equinox Publishing Ltd, 2011), hardback, xxxii + 640 pp., ISBN: 978-1-84553-166-9, US$ 80.00.

    Chas. H. Barfoot should be thanked for writing an essential volume on the life and ministry of Aimee Semple McPherson. She was much endeared by her followers. She affectionately stated her relationship with them that "to the world, I might be Aimee, but to my own dear people I am 'Sister.'"(477) "'Sister Aimee,' as she would fondly be called," (2) the founder of the International Church of the Foursquare Gospel, is perceptively and vividly depicted in Barfoot's colorful biography. Barfoot painted a portrait of Sister Aimee. He produced an interpretation of her life. The author has placed his research during the early years of the Pentecostal movement. His vast knowledge of the Pentecostal tradition that Sister Aimee has spearheaded and influenced is clearly evident in *Aimee Semple McPherson and the Making of Modern Pentecostalism 1890-1926*. Barfoot has produced a documentation of her scandalous life. The author also chronicled a readable story of her celebrated preaching career. However, he did not generate a strict academic writing about Sister Aimee. Rather, he delivers with a blending of rigorously studied public records and anecdotal materials, familiar events and journalistic accounts as well as personal letters and archive resources.

    The many black and white photos in the pages of the book bring to life the narrative text. Barfoot's presentation of this lady preacher is between the scholarly and the tabloid. Although, he keeps away from a popular hagiography and employs the historical framework of the Pentecostal revival, nonetheless, he has a subjective tendency of putting his personal knowledge and love for Sister Aimee in his prose. This use of personal note is not to be taken as a negative at all. It is a writing style that is distinctive and can be treated as more valuable in writing a life story of a remarkable woman. It is notable that he prevents himself from magnifying the scandals or focusing on the idealistic. Reasonably, Barfoot attempts to capture a picture of a lady preacher in her elusiveness. The author is optimistic about the contribution of Sister Aimee to contemporary Pentecostalism and American life: "By ingeniously uniting as one both the sacred and secular, she became the movement's most glamorous symbol of success and its most visible spokesperson. An innovative and charismatic leader, she charted the course and blazed the trail for the movement's future." (xxiii)

Sister Aimee understood the American culture. She capitalized on it. She did not shy away from the combining of the spiritual and the nonspiritual. She made the Pentecostal expression of faith tolerable to the taste of the mainline Protestants of America. Barfoot has that sense of strong connection with Aimee Semple McPherson. The reader will not miss the respect and affection of the author as he resurrected Sister Aimee in his book. It is not only his academic background and proficient qualification as well as his family upbringing and religious heritage that made him competent to write this valuable biography but most of all there is that continuity that he embodies in himself with her. The author's preface and acknowledgments show his sympathy and attachment to Sister Aimee. Her story is his story. The writing of her biography is telling the story that must be told! And so, Barfoot tells the story of Aimee Semple McPherson in twenty-one chapters. These chapters are entertaining. It is hard not to be ardently affected and sympathetically attached to this remarkable woman of faith as one gets to know her through the pen of Barfoot. The reviewer is carried emotionally by the ups and downs of Sister Aimee. The author is very sympathetic to her. The biographical details, the names and circumstances of people around her, the concurrent historical events that happened during her lifetime and the insightful commentaries are beautifully woven together.

Barfoot starts with her birth during the autumn of 1890 (October 9, 1890) in a Canadian farm and at the same time talks about her funeral in October 1944 in the first page of chapter one. She was born as Aimee Elizabeth Kennedy, lived a short but significant life, and died as a sophisticated woman. (1) After some details on the circumstances of her early life and the significant influence of her parents until she met Robert Semple (2 ff.), the narrative moves to Sister Aimee's love life and subsequent marriage to this Pentecostal "preacher who died young in the second chapter." In chapter three, Sister Aimee's Jonah syndrome has been highlighted after the death of her first husband Robert Semple, the birth of her daughter Roberta Star Kennedy Semple and her subsequent remarriage to Harold McPherson that brought Rolf Potter Kennedy McPherson into this life. The next two chapters talk about the thriving ministry of the McPhersons and the sad story of their parting of ways. The sixth and seventh chapters transport the story of Sister Aimee's life to California, underlining her connections to Los Angeles and Azusa Street. "The Beautiful Woman in White" is the title of the following chapter because Sister Aimee "was remembered" as "being 'very good looking and she dressed always in a white uniform.'" (161) This chapter also mentions how Sister Aimee influenced Hollywood celebrities like Jean Harlow, Marilyn Monroe,

Anthony Quinn and Charlie Chaplin. (172) In chapters nine, ten and eleven the accounts of Barfoot demonstrate how Sister Aimee was daring enough to walk in between the sacred and the secular, "popular religious culture" and "high church culture" as well as the Pentecostal practice and high class church.

The next half of the volume maps the geographical success and the notable impression of Sister Aimee in the American society of her time and also her scandalous disappearance and return. The succeeding seven chapters highlight the locations in the United States where Sister Aimee made lasting impact. They are San Diego, California, Denver, Colorado, Northern California, Rochester, New York, Wichita, Kansas, Oakland, California and Angelus Temple in Los Angeles, California. The subsequent chapter is a chronicle of how Pentecostalism has come to the American Protestants, particularly the Methodists, wherein Sister Aimee served as a bridge. (421-428) The title of chapter twenty is "May 18, 1926." After describing the different success stories of Sister Aimee, the author relate the circumstances of the news that the famous lady preacher was drowned and her remains were not found. (455 ff.) The last chapter explains her vanishing because of her alleged abduction and her later appearance on June 23, 1926 in Douglas, Arizona.

In his epilogue, Barfoot reflects on the testimonial experiences of people, the historical appropriation of religion in the society and the pursuit of genuine spiritual encounter. His insight is thought provoking: ". . . Pentecostalism is thriving today, and religion is still with us, because for many people, it simply works." (529) The story of such a remarkable woman who contributed so much to the Pentecostal movement is still with us today. What she has started still works for today. Her contribution to the Pentecostal faith should be understood as a source of inspiration and strength. *Aimee Semple McPherson and the Making of Modern Pentecostalism 1890-1926* is not only an enjoyable read but also an important spiritual reminder and a human challenge. God chooses to use flawed people.

R. G. dela Cruz

Lian Xi, *Redeemed by Fire: The Rise of Popular Christianity in Modern China* (New Haven: Yale University Press, 2010).

Lian Xi has produced a remarkably detailed, skillfully written, and meticulously researched history of important indigenous Christian movements and leaders in modern China. Focusing on the period from the early 1900s to the present, Xi covers the True Jesus Church, the Jesus Family, the Shandong revivals and leaders such as John Sung, Wang Mingdao, and Watchman Nee, to name a few. He also offers detailed analysis of more recent house church movements and a number of the contemporary cults.

In spite of the obvious strengths of this book and the intellectual gifts of its author, this study is marred by a number of weaknesses. These weaknesses are all related to the author's presuppositions. Xi often writes in condescending tones when he describes the millenarian or apocalyptic views of his subjects. He appears to judge these "popular" movements, rooted as they are in apocalyptic visions of the future, in Marxist-like terms as serving as an "opiate" that dulls the pain of the harsh realities faced by the poor and oppressed. The eschatological views of these groups—almost all of them look to the future for a radical transformation of the present order—are often ridiculed or dismissed as utopian and naive in Xi's narrative. Additionally, he links these views with Pentecostal ecstasies (healing, exorcism, visions, and speaking in tongues), and paints these groups as rooted in syncretistic practices driven by their context of poverty and oppression. However, Xi's analysis misses a number of important elements.

First, Xi fails to recognize or acknowledge that these eschatological views and Pentecostal practices are all found in the early church and the Bible, especially the book of Acts. In other words, these groups are generally orthodox and Evangelical in character (Xi doesn't make a strong distinction between orthodox, Evangelical groups and those that are cultic) and reflect views and practices shared by millions (some would say the majority) of Christians around the world. The biblical background for these beliefs and practices is rarely noted and never highlighted; rather, there is constant reference to similar practices or concepts in Chinese religions. Yet, it is quite evident that the Bible has profoundly impacted these groups and that the loose parallels in other religions merely indicate that these practices address felt needs, like in so many other countries and cultures around the world.[1]

---

[1] For example, without any reference to the biblical pedigree of Pentecostal belief and practice (see especially the book of Acts) and the fact that these beliefs and practices are also featured by hundreds of millions of Christians around the world, Xi writes:

Xi also appears to dismiss apocalyptic and millenarian eschatological views as escapist and, at best, irrelevant. Here he fails to acknowledge that these views have been a part of the Christian faith from the earliest of days (most would trace them back to Jesus), are firmly rooted in the Bible, and have left an extremely positive legacy. Although it might appear counter-intuitive, people with a strong faith in the second coming of Jesus have been empowered and active in alleviating and transforming lives and societies in the present world. A strong and clear vision of the future enables Christians to live moral and heroic lives of service in this present age.[2] The escapist narrative so often touted by sociologists and not a few theologians simply is not accurate and needs to be challenged.

The same might be said for Xi's dismissal of "Pentecostal ecstasies" (to use his term). His reductionistic perspective also blinds him to the incredibly positive legacy left by a century of Pentecostal pioneers. According to Xi, Pentecostal manifestations such as healings, exorcisms, visions, and tongues, like the apocalyptic views noted above, are symptoms generated by a life of deprivation and impoverishment. But this judgment, which was often championed by a previous generation of sociologists, is now tired and outdated. It has been proven to be based on faulty premises (these experiences are the result of poverty and oppression) and simply does not accurately reflect the current data available.[3] More importantly, it misses the incredible impact that the Pentecostal faith is having on the faithful around the world. As sociologist David Martin notes, Pentecostals are having a tremendous impact among the poor of Latin American precisely because of the clarity of their message, rooted in the Bible. With reference to the challenges facing poor families in Brazil, which are often ravaged by the pull of "a culture of machismo, drink, sexual conquest, and carnival," Martin writes: "It is a contest between the

---

"Instead of bringing back to life withered Western faith, the Chinese were fashioning a Christian faith that increasingly revealed continuities with indigenous folk religion, which also made a startling comeback during the same period, attracting some two hundred million worshippers at the turn of the twenty-first century" (*Redeemed by Fire*, 230).

[2]David Martin aptly notes, "Pentecostals belong to groups which liberals cast in the role of victim, and in every way they refuse to play that role." (*Pentecostalism: The World Their Parish* [Oxford: Blackwell, 2002], 10). Although it often goes unrecognized, Pentecostals around the globe are having a dramatic social impact. But they are doing so precisely because they are focused on a clear biblical message of repentance, forgiveness, transformation, and hope.

[3]For example, Max Turner writes, "Contrary to earlier claims, there is no evidence that 'tongues speech' is correlated with low intellect, education, social position or pathological psychology." (*The Holy Spirit and Spiritual Gifts: Then and Now* [Carlisle: Paternoster, 1996], 305). See also the numerous studies he cites.

home and the street, and what restores the home is the discontinuity and inner transformation offered by a demanding, disciplined faith with firm boundaries."[4]

All of this blunts Xi's ability to see these Christian groups as having much to contribute to China's future. Here again we encounter another questionable assumption: if these groups do not directly impact those with political power, they are irrelevant and have little to offer. While it is probably accurate to say that the vast majority of China's Christians will not coalesce into a unified, powerful political block, their potential for impacting China's future should not be underestimated. Indeed, their message of the worth of each individual, a firm moral compass, purpose beyond selfish interests, and hope for the future has the potential to dramatically impact a nation in search of meaning.

Robert P. Menzies

---

[4]Martin, *The World Their Parish*, 105-6.

Contributing Editors to This Edition

Aldrin M. Peñamora, Ph.D. is currently serving as Research Manager on Christian-Muslim Relations under the Philippine Council of Evangelical Churches (PCEC). He is a visiting faculty of Asian Theological Seminary, and taught at Kononia Theological Seminary in Davao City. During his doctoral studies at Fuller Theological Seminary, Aldrin's sincere interest in Christian-Muslim peacemaking in Mindanao grew under the mentorship of the late theological ethicist and originator of the "just peacemaking" paradigm, Dr. Glen H. Stassen.

Yuri Phanon, M.Div, is a graduate of APTS and is currently living in the Philippines with her husband, Anattiphong (K), who is pursuing an MTh at APTS.

Ivan Satyavrata, Ph.D, is the pastor of the Buntain Memorial Church in Kolkata, India, and travels and speaks internationally.

Al Tizon, Ph.D, is Executive Minister of Serve Globally, the international ministries of the Evangelical Covenant Church, and Affiliate Professor of Missional and Global Leadership at North Park Theological Seminary, both located in Chicago, IL He is an ordained minister with the Evangelical Covenant Church and has engaged in community development work and church leadership development both in the Philippines and the United States.

www.ingramcontent.com/pod-product-compliance
Lightning Source LLC
Chambersburg PA
CBHW070936160426
43193CB00011B/1705